"This is a splendid primer on the legendary work of James Masterson. In this scholarly yet accessible introduction, Loray Daws shows the chronology of his mentor's novel contributions to understanding borderline, narcissistic, and schizoid phenomena; and is able to distill with supple elegance the complex developmental and clinical theories Masterson contributed to articulating and treating disorders of the self. An essential read for those working with character pathology."

Professor Jon Mills, *Department of Psychosocial & Psychoanalytic Studies, University of Essex, and author of* Psyche, Culture, World: Excursions in Existentialism and Psychoanalytic Philosophy *(Routledge, 2022)*

"James Masterson, MD., created foundational concepts in understanding and treating personality disorders. In authoring this book, Loray Daws, a preeminent practitioner of the Masterson approach, provides essentials. Masterson will stand in history as one of psychotherapy's luminous voices. His work guides my practice."

Jeffrey K Zeig, *Ph.D., The Milton H. Erickson Foundation; Architect of the Evolution of Psychotherapy Conferences*

"Dr. Daws offers far more than an introductory primer, this book is a passionate, detailed, and remarkable rendering of the breadth and scope of James Masterson's significant psychoanalytic theoretical/clinical contributions (along with Masterson's associates) coupled with the author's compelling story of a clinician's journey to find the deepest understanding of the human experience. Dr. Daws fluidly manages the diverse notions of psychoanalytic developmental/object relations theory with an eye toward blending theory, with true-to-life clinical examples, displaying that rare combination of astute technical acumen while sustaining approachable humanistic observations of the very nature of psychoanalytic treatment."

Jack Schwartz, *PsyD, NCPsyA, Training analyst/Faculty New Jersey Institute and Object Relations Institute, writer and lecturer*

James F. Masterson

In this volume, Loray Daws traces the life and work of Dr. James F. Masterson, with a focus on the scientific development and later expansion of the six developmental stages of the Masterson Method.

Exploring more than 15 of Masterson's volumes, as well as countless articles, Daws shows how Masterson's approach to Object Relations and the developmental self can serve clinicians in both conceptualizing and treating borderline, narcissistic, and schizoid disorders of self. Considering the pioneering and innovative nature of Masterson's work, Daws looks at how he creatively expanded on Freud's theories on repression, successfully developing therapeutically sound ways to touch and transform developmental trauma and trauma reflected in a deep abandonment depression.

James F. Masterson: A Contemporary Introduction will be of interest to students in psychology, psychiatry, and psychiatric nursing, as well as psychoanalytically orientated psychotherapists, psychoanalysts, and those specializing in the ever-growing field of the treatment of the disorders of the self.

Loray Daws is a registered clinical psychologist in South Africa and British Columbia, Canada. He is currently in private practice and serves both as a senior faculty member at the International Masterson Institute and as a board member at the Object Relations Institute in New York. Loray specializes in psychoanalysis and daseinsanalysis, and he is the editor of five books on psychoanalysis and existential analysis.

Routledge Introductions to Contemporary Psychoanalysis

Aner Govrin, Ph.D.
Series Editor

Yael Peri Herzovich, Ph.D.
Executive Editor

Itamar Ezer
Assistant Editor

"Routledge Introductions to Contemporary Psychoanalysis" is one of the prominent psychoanalytic publishing ventures of our day. It will comprise dozens of books that will serve as concise introductions dedicated to influential concepts, theories, leading figures, and techniques in psychoanalysis covering every important aspect of psychoanalysis.

The length of each book is fixed at 40,000 words.

The series' books are designed to be easily accessible to provide informative answers in various areas of psychoanalytic thought. Each book will provide updated ideas on topics relevant to contemporary psychoanalysis – from the unconscious and dreams, projective identification and eating disorders, through neuropsychoanalysis, colonialism, and spiritual-sensitive psychoanalysis. Books will also be dedicated to prominent figures in the field, such as Melanie Klein, Jacques Lacan, Sándor Ferenczi, Otto Kernberg, and Michael Eigen.

Not serving solely as an introduction for beginners, the purpose of the series is to offer compendiums of information on particular topics within different psychoanalytic schools. We ask authors to review a topic but also address the readers with their own personal views and contribution to the specific chosen field. Books will make intricate ideas comprehensible without compromising their complexity.

We aim to make contemporary psychoanalysis more accessible to both clinicians and the general educated public.

Aner Govrin – Editor

Sigmund Freud: A Contemporary Introduction
Susan Sugarman

Marion Milner: A Contemporary Introduction
Alberto Stefana and Alessio Gamba

James F. Masterson: A Contemporary Introduction
Loray Daws

James F. Masterson

A Contemporary Introduction

Loray Daws

Routledge
Taylor & Francis Group
LONDON AND NEW YORK

Designed cover image: © Michal Heiman, Asylum 1855-2020, The Sleeper (video, psychoanalytic sofa and Plate 34), exhibition view, Herzliya Museum of Contemporary Art, 2017.

First published 2024
by Routledge
4 Park Square, Milton Park, Abingdon, Oxon OX14 4RN

and by Routledge
605 Third Avenue, New York, NY 10158

Routledge is an imprint of the Taylor & Francis Group, an informa business

British Library Cataloguing-in-Publication Data
A catalogue record for this book is available from the British Library

ISBN: 978-1-032-41537-6 (hbk)
ISBN: 978-1-032-41536-9 (pbk)
ISBN: 978-1-003-35857-2 (ebk)

DOI: 10.4324/9781003358572

Typeset in Times New Roman
by Deanta Global Publishing Services, Chennai, India

Contents

Foreword

James F. Masterson: A Contemporary Introduction

James F. Masterson, psychoanalytic psychiatrist, spearheaded a critical shift in the thought and practice of the mental health field. From a predominant focus on symptoms, the perspective of healing was widened to a concern with the whole self, and especially the self in relationship with others. Concurrently with pioneering colleagues such as Kernberg, Kohut, and Searles, Masterson brought into focus a new therapeutic challenge: understanding and treatment of the personality disorders that characterize the psychic dislocation of our time. First, having created an effective therapeutic approach to the "untreatable" borderline patient, Masterson then formed a dynamic synthesis of psychoanalytic psychotherapy that addressed the full range of personality disorders, or disorders of the self as he came to refer to them. In time, Masterson extended his range of treatment and teaching beyond his New York City office complex to an international Institute that networked among centers on the West Coast (USA), Canada, South Africa, Australia, and Turkey. Those of us who Masterson taught were invited to become part of the Institute, and, in turn, to participate in an ongoing process of therapeutic service to patients and trainees that is now entering its third generation.

Loray Daws, a long-term, devoted participant in Masterson's achievements, brings us an introduction to Masterson's work that is both comprehensive and highly readable. He contributes years of immediate experience and knowledge to this skilled presentation of Masterson's thought and practice: a founding father of the South African and British Columbia Masterson Institutes, he is also a faculty member of the International Masterson Institute, NY, and the Object

Relations Institute in New York, where he teaches Masterson's therapeutic approach to the disorders of the self. In addition, his facility with the written word allows us to go beyond the concepts to share the warmth of his feelings for Masterson as teacher and mentor.

This Foreword would not be complete without a personal note. My relationship with Loray, as a colleague and friend, spans much of the growth of Masterson's Institute. It has been a creative, dizzying procession of classes, workshops, and conferences on different continents and in varying time zones and venues. Throughout, Loray's astonishing energy and enthusiasm have only been matched by his dedication to learning and teaching. Our journey together began under the tutelage of Masterson himself, and Loray now continues that tradition with this accomplished tribute to a dynamic originator in the field of mental health.

Candace Orcutt, M.A., Ph.D.
Psychoanalyst
Former Associate, James Masterson

Acknowledgments

My deepest gratitude to Aner Govrin and Tair Caspi for supporting the current work by including James Masterson in the *Routledge Introduction to Contemporary Psychoanalysis*.

The Masterson Institute – my home for more than 16 years. Most notably, Dr. Judith Pearson, Director of the International Masterson Institute, who made training at the Institute possible in the mid-2000s through remote technology. Also, Dr. James Masterson, Candace Orcutt, Murray Schane, Jerry Katz, and my colleagues Mr. William Griffith, Daleen Macklin, Paul Shiel, and Caroline Bankston for background support.

My editor, Ms. Jana Craddock, for your enthusiastic support and attention to detail.

My analysts, Dr. Assie Gildenhuys, Dr. A.C.N. Preller, and Ms. Janet Oakes – forever accompanying me in guarding the Real Self.

Dr. Ann-Marie Lydall and Mr. JP Theron, senior Masterson clinicians and Faculty of the International Masterson Institute, for the clinical material in Chapters 5 and 6.

Special thank you to Courtenay Young, editor-in-chief of the *International Journal of Psychotherapy*, for permission to use sections from the following publication: Daws, L. 2012. The Use of Distancing, Avoidance, and Focusing on the Object as Defenses in the Borderline Disorder of Self – A Mastersonian Approach. *International Journal of Psychotherapy*, 16(1), 18–29.

Special thank you to the BC Association of Clinical Counsellors' Insights into Clinical Counselling for reproducing sections taken from Daws, L. 2011. *The Mastersonian Approach to the Borderline Disorder of Self*, Daws, L. 2011. *Ghostliners: The Mastersonian Approach to the Schizoid Disorder of Self*, and Daws, L. 2013. *Living between Omnipotence and Deflation: A Mastersonian View of the Narcissistic Dilemma.*

The following two journals are no longer in print, and although all attempts were made to obtain permission, no correspondence has been received to date. Nonetheless, I fully acknowledge *The Journal of Contemporary Psychotherapy* for using sections of the following publications; Daws, L. 2011. Grandiosity and Perfection: The Mastersonian Approach to the Narcissistic Disorders of the Self. *Contemporary Psychotherapy*, 3(2). http://contemporarypsychotherapy.org/volume-3-no-2-winter-2011/grandiosity-and-perfection/; Daws, L. 2013. Living between Rewarding and Withdrawing Paradigms of Experience: The Mastersonian Approach to the Borderline Disorder of Self. *Contemporary Psychotherapy*. http://contemporarypsychotherapy.org/volume-4-no-2-winter-2012/living-between-rewarding-and-withdrawing-paradigms-of-experience/; Daws, L. 2013. Is There Anybody Out There? The Mastersonian Approach to the Schizoid Dilemma. *Contemporary Psychotherapy*. http://contemporarypsychotherapy.org/volume-5-no-1-spring-2013/is-there-anybody-out-there, and the *Journal of Psychoanalytic Psychology* (Washington Square Institute, N.Y., closed) for Daws, L. 2009. Dreaming the Dream: In Search of Endopsychic Ontology. *Issues in Psychoanalytic Psychology*, 31(1), 21–40.

Finally, Dr. Jeffrey Zeig, editor-in-chief of Zeig-Tucker & Thiesen, for permission to reproduce the split units as they appeared in Masterson and Lieberman (2004) and Keri Cohen, Daleen Macklin, and Dr. Candance Orcutt for reading the manuscript and for conceptual and editorial support.

Part I

Meeting James Masterson and the Importance of the Developmental Self and Object Relations Approach in Psychoanalysis and Treatment of the Pre-Oedipal Analysand

Core Concepts

Chapter 1

The Developmental Self and Object Relations Approach of James F. Masterson

Masterson Over the Years – A Personal Reflection and Introduction

I first encountered Dr. James F. Masterson's unique developmental self and object relations approach during my M.A. in Clinical Psychology while preparing to write a research proposal on Burning Mouth Syndrome (BMS). Studying the pioneering work of Dr. P.A. Botha at the Department of Periodontology at the University of Pretoria, then serving as my thesis supervisor, I became increasingly interested in finding psychoanalytically informed developmental language to explain the inner world of BMS patients. In reviewing the process of separation-individuation described by Dr. Masterson in *Disorders of the Self – New Therapeutic Horizons* (1995), I instantly knew I had discovered a novel way of conceptualizing the separation-individuation difficulties in BMS patients. Not only did Masterson's thinking and theorizing open up new theoretical vertices, but clinically Masterson's Developmental Self and Object Relations Approach introduced me to an innovative way of *being present* to analysands struggling with pre-Oedipal defenses and deficits. In the description of the psychoanalyst Dr. Calvin F. Settlage, "the patient's use of the analyst as a developmental object can be enhanced by *adding* a *developmental stance* to the usual psychoanalytic stance" (Settlage, in Akhtar, 2001, pp. 88–89). It was not until December 25, 2005, while searching for further training in psychoanalysis, that I came across the Masterson Institute in New York. I enthusiastically emailed Dr. Judith Pearson, the Director of Training, who, unbeknownst to me, was an avid traveler already well acquainted with South Africa and Africa in general. At the invitation of Dr. Pearson and Masterson, William Griffith and I set off to meet the faculty in August 2006. By January 2007, we

DOI: 10.4324/9781003358572-2

gathered a small cohort that included various South Africans such as Paul Shiel, Daleen Macklin, William Griffith, myself, and Carolyne Bankston in Florida, USA. Yearly conferences and travel to New York followed weekly seminars until our matriculation in January 2010. Although blessed to receive group supervision from Dr. Masterson and partake in many conversations on clinical technique and process, Dr. Masterson died of pneumonia on April 12, 2010, at 84. It was a true privilege to experience supervision with him, his humor, and his sensitivity to the patient's deep psychic struggle on the road to wholeness. I will never forget his gentle voice when he echoed, "Never forget Loray, the patients we work with are fighting for their psychic survival – we serve as guardians to the Real Self." For me, Dr. Masterson's work serves as a *Guardian to the Real Self* – for those we serve who have been exposed to developmental processes unable to support the autochthonous I.

Evolution of the Masterson Approach

According to Dr. Masterson, the Masterson Approach evolved from observing, empathizing, and clinically adapting to the various separation-individuation difficulties his analysands faced. Although early Masterson mainly remained perplexed by multiple forms of *adolescent turmoil* and, at times, the relative laissez-faire psychiatric approach ("they will grow out of it") to their difficulty, the Masterson Approach developed through various stages to encompass both adolescent and adult forms of disorders of self. Masterson himself mentioned that his work could be read as a progression through six stages, starting in the late 1950s to his last publication in 2005.

In stage one, the psychiatric dilemma of adolescence (1956–1968), we meet a young psychoanalytically orientated psychiatrist caught in his *own identity struggle* as a researcher and clinician. Dr. Masterson described it as follows:

> What I did not realize at the time was that (a) I was now flirting with becoming a methodological researcher and relegating the intrapsychic and psychodynamic to the background as a means of dealing with my own intrapsychic problems; (b) I had made a decision to undertake a project from which it would take me 12 years (from 1956 to 1968) to extricate myself, and (c) when *I emerged*, the *temptation to use work as a resistance to understanding my own*

> *intrapsychic problems would have been resolved with the crystallization of a unified, harmonious perspective on both the inner and the outer, on my self and on my work...*A conflict began to grow in me between the social science methodological point of view, and the clinical point of view, which emphasizes the importance of considering all variables at one time and sees clinical judgment as the only final instrument of observation and decision. At the same time, in my personal analysis I was delving deeper and deeper into my own psyche. I would spend three hours a day at the clinic trying to refine methodology... — and then go to an analytic session that would repeatedly demonstrate how often these activities served as well to reinforce my resistance to facing my own emotional problems.
>
> (1989, pp. xii–xiii) (italics added)

According to Masterson, his creative conflict was finally resolved during a conference where he settled on a clinical point of view rather than the statistical, and at "the same time my use of work as a resistance to my own intrapsychic problems diminished dramatically" (1989, p. xiii). Not that the statistical approach did not advance the field of adolescent developmental difficulty, and in 1967, the book *The Psychiatric Dilemma of Adolescence* was published, wherein Dr. Masterson found that adolescents did not "grow out of it." Even more seriously, five years after evaluation, more than 50% of the adolescents evaluated remained severely impaired. Dr. Masterson's research also found that weekly treatment over a year did alleviate various symptoms (such as anxiety, depression, and acting out); however, the therapies relied upon did not touch *core development difficulties*, and as such, adaptation remained compromised across various domains.[1] During this time, Masterson was asked to serve as head of the adolescent in-patient unit at the Payne Whitney Clinic, an opportune environment allowing Masterson to observe more closely the developmental difficulties disorder of self adolescents experienced. These observations would later become the bedrock of the Masterson Approach.

During 1968–1974, the second stage of development, Dr. Masterson set up a research unit for the intensive psychoanalytic psychotherapy of adolescent behavioral disorders. Receiving institutional support, the adolescents could reside for at least a year in the clinic setting, and a psychiatric resident would remain in service to the adolescent for that period. The hospitalized adolescents continuously challenged the clinical frame with, at times, rather severe acting out, necessitating the development of limit setting[2] of this much-needed but restrictive defense/adaptation mechanism. Surviving the adolescent's "trial by fire" (1989, p. xiv) profoundly affected the adolescents and the treatment team as it became clear that as the adolescents contained and controlled their behavior, they became exceedingly *depressed*. So the first and fundamental link in Masterson's thinking crystallized: acting out may be viewed as a needed defense against depression!

The *source* of the depression initially eluded Dr. Masterson, although conflicts surrounding emancipation seemed rather obvious. Dr. Masterson faithfully returned to various analysts such as Anna Freud, Peter Blos, P. Greenacre, and E.H. Erikson to solve the riddle and be of therapeutic use to the struggling and depressed adolescent inpatients. Serendipitously, as Dr. Masterson scanned through journals, the psychoanalytic work of émigré' Margaret Mahler spoke directly to Masterson's observations. Although the article Masterson read focussed mainly on psychotic children,[3] the research did introduce Masterson to Mahler's foundational thinking on the development of the self through the various stages of separation-individuation (SI). Dr. Masterson also writes that as he was studying the work of Mahler and her colleagues, his adolescent patients increasingly opened up about their painful conflicts with their parents. Shared memories seemed to reflect earlier separation-individuation challenges (SI), specifically, the mother's conflicts around the SI needs of their children's emerging or individuating self:

> It dawned on me that, again serendipitously, I was in the midst of two complementary research experiments. In other words, Mahler's work educated me about the early development of the normal self while my own adolescent patients were describing and demonstrating dramatically the failures of that normal process, the developmental arrest of the self of the borderline personality disorder. I put the two together, which led to the view that the borderline personality disorder was a developmental problem—a failure in separation-individuation or in development of the self.
>
> (1989, p. xv)

For Masterson, a piece of the puzzle fell into place that would later be known as the borderline disorder of self, wherein maternal unavailability and lack of acknowledgment of the self are reflected in an abandonment depression serving, in part, as a reason for the developmental arrest of the ego. This understanding also highlighted the often-misunderstood therapeutic technique of *confrontation*:[4] the active mentalization of the adolescent's defenses against his separation-individuation conflicts and abandonment depression. For Masterson, the latter therapeutic approach is expected to lead to the working through of the abandonment depression, freeing the *developmental self* to resume the separation-individuation process. The findings of this period were published in 1972 in the book *Treatment of the Borderline Adolescent: A Developmental Approach.* To Masterson's surprise, if not dismay, the book was met with thundering silence.[5] It was only after the second book, *Psychotherapy of the Borderline Adult* (1976), was published that the first book received considerable attention. Despite painful beginnings and a lack of peer and environmental resonance, many questions remained for Masterson. Most its object relations speak of all was the complex relationship between intrapsychic structure, developmental arrest, and maternal unavailability. Focussing on this area limed the third stage of Masterson's work (1974–1983), a most creative period consolidating his professional development as a psychoanalytic psychiatrist with a unique focus on the developmental object relations approach to character disorders in adolescents and adults. Serendipitously, Dr. Masterson's focus on the intrapsychic development of the borderline dilemma cultivated a unique friendship with the great Dr. Donald Rinsley, a creative and clinically astute Fairbairnian thinker. Their innovative conceptualizations can be read in the 1975 article entitled "The Borderline Syndrome: The Role of the Mother in the Genesis and Psychic Structure of the Borderline Personality," published in *The International Journal of Psychoanalysis*, and expanded upon in various volumes such as *The Psychotherapy of the Borderline Adult: A Developmental Approach* in 1976, the follow-up study (with Dr. Jacinta Lu Costello) on the adolescents treated in the in-patient unit reflected in the book *From Borderline Adolescent to Functioning Adult: The Test of Time* in 1980, *The Narcissistic and Borderline Disorders: A Developmental Approach* in 1981, and *Countertransference and Psychotherapeutic Technique* in 1983. The professional accomplishments also find Masterson's own separation-individuation process reflected in his growing focus and confidence in his clinical work with character disorders, the effectiveness of his developmental model, and peer recognition supported him in leaving Cornell and creating his own organization, the Masterson Group for the treatment of personality disorders, and the Masterson Institute, a non-profit training institution for both teaching and research in developmental psychoanalysis.

During the forming years, a memorable conference was held at Hunter College, New York, on November 5, 1977, which included papers and discussions by pre-eminent thinkers such as Peter L. Giovacchini, Otto F. Kernberg, and Harold F. Searles and was published in *New Perspectives on Psychotherapy of the Borderline Adult* (1978), contrasting various viewpoints from pioneers in the field. Interestingly, after a prosperous decade of exploration, rich conceptualizations, and professional success, Dr. Masterson noted that by 1983 he felt his writing days might be over! Clinically, Masterson remained unsatisfied with the developmental object relations theory's approach to the *Self*,

> I found myself without intention or plan focussing more and more in my work with my patients on the patient's self, to the point of spontaneously developing a symbol (S) for when the patient was activating his real self in the session, and (O) for his relationship with object.
>
> (1989, p. xix)

Masterson's further differentiation and articulation of the *Real Self* in relation to the *defensive self* brought the developmental self and object relations approach "to a kind of fullness or completeness appropriate to the demands of the clinical material" (1989, p. xiv). Dr. Masterson's work on the *Real Self* and his struggle to articulate its presence in the analytic process can be read in *The Real Self: A Developmental, Self, and Object Relations Approach,* published in 1985, as well as a very accessible book for a more general non-clinical audience, entitled *The Search for the Real Self: Unmasking the Personality Disorders of Our Age,* published in 1988.

The fifth stage, 1988–1996, found a creative deepening of the Masterson Approach. As Masterson himself notes in the preface of his edited work *Psychotherapy of the Disorders of Self: The Masterson Approach* (with Ralph Klein, 1989), "The Masterson Approach has evolved from 32 years of scientific inquiry, including four formal research projects, nine books, and 75 papers" (p. vii). Works such as *The Emerging Self: A Developmental Self & Object Relations Approach To The Treatment of the Closet Narcissistic Disorder of the Self*, in 1993, and *Disorders of Self: New Therapeutic Horizons* in 1995 (with R. Klein) showcased senior faculty members such as Ralph Klein, M.D, Candace Orcutt, Ph.D., Shelley Barlas Nagel, Ph.D., Karla Clark, Ph.D., Richard Fischer, Ph.D., and Judith Pearson, Ph.D., all significantly contributing to a deepening of the approach as well as adding further structural thinking by integrating Fairbairnian and Guntripian thinking on the schizoid disorder on self (Ralph Klein), the importance of understanding trauma and post-traumatic stress disorder on the development of disorders of the self and its impact on general technique (Dr. Orcutt), and finding creative ways in working with entrenched states of mind such as found in extreme devaluation, helplessness, hopelessness, despair, terror, and desuetude. To add to the work of the faculty and the expanding method, two workshops held on February 23–24 1990, in New York, and March 9–10, 1990, in San Francisco, California, with well-known short-term psychoanalytic practitioners and self-psychologists culminated in a volume entitled *Comparing Psychoanalytic Psychotherapies: Developmental, Self, and Object Relations, Self Psychology, Short-Term Dynamic*, with esteem clinician-scholars Drs Marian Tolpin and Peter E. Sifneos (1991).

In the 2000s, Dr. Masterson ushered the method's sixth stage (1995) with three publications. The *Personality Disorders: An Update on the Developmental Self and Object Relations Approach to Diagnosis and Treatment* (2002) found Dr. Masterson reflecting on his developmental self and object relations theory as standing the test of time. Given the growing scientific interest in the empirically validated work of John Bowlby's attachment theory and the neurobiological work of Allan Schore, various studies empirically demonstrated the importance of maternal availability in forming a secure attachment. Stage six not only critically reviewed the basic tenets of the Masterson Approach but also focussed on writing a concise guide and workbook for clinicians, *A Therapist Guide to the Personality Disorders – The Masterson Approach: A Handbook and Workbook* (2004, with A.R. Lieberman). Masterson's last edited book, *The Personality Disorders Through the Lens of Attachment Theory and the Neurobiologic Development of the Self: A Clinical Integration* (2005), effectively integrates attachment theory with neurobiology, furthering Masterson's central tenets concerning the role of the mother.

Masterson's work also found creative roots in both independent Mastersonians and non-Masterson-trained clinicians using Masterson's thinking to further their innovative models of mind. Here we see the work of Donald D. Roberts and Deanda S. Roberts, *Another Chance to Be Real: Attachment and Object Relations Treatment of Borderline Personality Disorder*, published in 2007, as well as the creative contributions of Kent Hoffman, Glen Cooper, and Bert Powell in their model "The Circle of Security," reflected in books such as *The Circle of Security Intervention: Enhancing Attachment in Early Parent-Child Relationships* in 2016 and *Raising a Secure Child: How Circle of Security Parenting Can Help You Nurture Your Child's Attachment, Emotional Resilience, and Freedom to Explore*, published in 2017. The NeuroAffective Relational Model (NARM) of Laurence Heller and colleagues also make clinical use of Masterson, as evident in their two volumes, *Healing Developmental Trauma: How Early Trauma Affects Self-Regulation, Self-Image, and The Capacity for Relationship* (2012), and *The Practical Guide for Healing Developmental Trauma: Using the NeuroAffective Relational Model to Address Adverse Childhood Experiences and Resolve Complex Trauma,* published in 2022. Another prolific couple therapist, Dr. Stan Tatkin, trained by Masterson, integrated Masterson's work into his approach called *A Psychobiological Approach to Couple Therapy* (PACT), and the couple therapy model of Ellyn Bader and Peter Pearson (1988) integrated both Mahler and Masterson's developmental thinking on separation-individuation to couples in crisis.

Finally, highly trained clinicians such as Elinor Greenberg, author of *Borderline, Narcissistic, and Schizoid Adaptations: The Pursuit of Love, Admiration, and Safety* (2016), and Patricia R. Frisch, author of *Whole Therapist, Whole Patient: Integrating Reich, Masterson, and Jung in Modern Psychotherapy* (2018), both build and expand on Masterson. However, no list would be complete without the contemporary psychoanalytic work of one of Masterson's most senior colleagues and contributor, Dr. Candace Orcutt, and her two volumes entitled *Trauma in Personality Disorders: A Clinician's Handbook – The Masterson Approach* (2012), and more recently, *The Unanswered Self: The Masterson Approach to the Healing of Personality Disorder* published in 2021. Dr. Masterson's work is also actively taught at the International Masterson Institute under Dr. Judith Pearson's directorship and has training institutes in America, Canada, South Africa, Turkey, and Australia. Psychoanalytic institutes, such as the Object Relations Institute in New York, teach and integrate Masterson's work with the work of analysts such as Susan Kavaler-Adler (1993, 1995, 2006, 2018) and her concept of *developmental mourning* in character disorders. With this publication, it is hoped, similar to the voice and thought of clinicians such as Harry Stack Sullivan (1953), another exceptional psychoanalytic thinker currently almost forgotten, that Masterson's personal and clinical struggles, thorough research, and personal sacrifice may not be overlooked.

The Relevance of Masterson's Approach to Modern Psychoanalytic Praxis

As will soon become evident, the Masterson Approach enables the clinician to integrate psychoanalytically derived concepts into formulating pre-Oedipal analysands' developmental (and thus intrapsychic) dilemmas, thereby constructing empirically sound clinical interventions to address these intrapsychic dilemmas, conflicts, and deficits. The chapters to come will explore in rich detail the clinical importance of developmental psychoanalytic thinking on analytic praxis, especially the work of Margaret Mahler (Chapter 2) in understanding the intrapsychic challenges and clinical needs of pre-Oedipal analysands. The challenges encountered in the various developmental phases of symbiosis and separation-individuation profoundly affect the self and object relationships formed intrapsychically, foreshadowing the reliance on defense mechanisms such as splitting and projective identification (Chapter 3). More specifically, developmental trauma can be found in all phases of development, each presenting a unique clinical picture, developmental need, and clinical approach, whether symbiotic (Chapter 4), withdrawn (the schizoid dilemma, Chapter 5), under the tyranny of fusion and omnipotence (narcissistic dilemma, Chapter 6), or reactive to separation stresses and strains (the borderline dilemma, Chapter 7). The volume will conclude with a synoptic reflection on the future of such an approach (Chapter 8).

Notes

1 Domains here would later fall under Masterson's "Real Self" concept that would include self-activation, self-agency, taking responsibility for self-activation, the capacity to soothe painful affect, and much more to be discussed in the upcoming chapters in greater detail.
2 Dr. Masterson mentions that he received much support and education from Dr. Willard Hendrickson, M.D., chief psychiatrist for many years at the University of Michigan adolescent unit.
3 Autism and Symbiosis: Two disturbances in the sense of entity and identity – see Mahler's collected papers, Volume 1, Chapter 9.

4 I will return to this concept in later chapters. It has been my experience that the word "confrontation" is an unfortunate one and being trained and supervised by Masterson, I became aware that its is everything but confrontational. Rather, what is meant by this technique is a rather active and relationally alive way of focussing and attending to contradiction and splits between thought, feeling, and behavior as an attempt to track the developmental triad, also to be discussed soon.

5 One could read in Masterson's description the importance of being met and its relationship to abandonment experiences; "This book, in retrospect, must have been way ahead of its time, as its appearance was greeted with thundering silence. I felt as if it had been dropped down a bottomless well. [an adandonment derivative]" (Masterson, 1989, p. xv).

Chapter 2

Growing Up, Away, Toward, Or Against – Masterson's Mahler

The Psychological Birth of the Human Infant – The Beginnings of Being and Becoming an I in Relation to Others

As mentioned in the opening chapter, early Masterson relied on Mahler and her colleagues to find developmental concepts able to explain and support the psychological turmoil endured by his adolescent patients as they navigated various familial and societal separation-individuation demands. Later Masterson, given his natural scientific attitude and uncanny ability to integrate scientific concepts in the psychiatric field into the clinical situation, found Masterson seamlessly integrating the work of Allan Schore, Mary Ainsworth, Donald Bowlby, Donald Stern, and many others with both Mahler and his observations. The progress of the Masterson approach can be viewed in greater detail in over 15 published academic and clinical volumes discussed in Chapter 1. For the aim of the current volume and chapters to come, I will remain committed to discussing Mahler's influence that supported Masterson's Developmental Self and Object relations model.[1] As a separation-individuation theory, Mahler and Masterson's psychoanalytic model proposed here focuses on the following:

- The importance of the pre-Oedipal period in psychological development.
- The analytic importance of self-object differentiation through various stages of development.
- The reality that all self-other differentiation arises from the complex interaction between mother and child.

DOI: 10.4324/9781003358572-3

- Conscious and unconscious knowledge/knowing of self and other is the product of self-other contact and the process of separation-individuation.
- Moving through separation-individuation implies a progressive loss (minimal loss, à la Settlage) of "participation of the parent in the child's regulatory and adaptive processes. These successive losses can be emotionally painful and sometimes are resisted. But the loss is counterbalanced by pleasure and satisfaction in the child's new achievement within developmental progression" (Settlage, in Kramer & Ahktar, 1994, p. 22).
- Separation-individuation, containing conscious and unconscious processes, is influenced by the mother's idiom toward her specific child. Since separation and individuation for Mahler can generally be viewed as two complementary developmental demands consisting of emerging (separation) from a symbiotic fusion with the mother and individuation, defined as the gathering of those developmental achievements indelibly "marking" the growing I's "assumption" of its own individual and subjective characteristics, great care must be given to the evolving and easily subverted I referred to by Masterson as the "Real Self." In Mahler's thinking, the implications for the practicing clinician are rather obvious,

> The birth of the child as an individual comes about when, in response to the mother's *selective response to his cuing*, the child *gradually alters his behavior*. The specific unconscious need of the mother *activates out of the infant's infinite potentialities*, those in particular that create for each mother "the child" who reflects her own unique and individual needs.[2] The process takes place, of course, within the range of the child's innate endowments.
>
> (Mahler, 1963, in Mahler et al., 1975, p. 60)

The work of Masterson and Winnicott[3] on the False Self, and the exceptional work of Brandscharf on *pathological accommodation* describe this "cuing" in much detail. Mutual cuing relies on a complex and ever-evolving process of both object relating and *object usage*,[4] as defined by Donald Winnicott and Christopher Bollas. "Objects" can "stimulate" the self in various ways: sensationally, structurally, conceptually/symbolically, mnemically, and protectively.

- The mother, throughout development, can be viewed to be in contact with and address not only the developmental phases as will soon be described but will also re-experience, consciously or otherwise, her own developmental gifts and limitations. During pre-Oedipal development, the mother must initially serve as a symbiotic organizer, followed by gently partnering the hatching process and, over time, serve as background support for both the practicing and rapprochement phases of development. Much of the developmental stages, themes, and conflicts will resurface through development, for many bringing a second opportunity to re-engage and rework areas of developmental conflict. Unfortunately, as will soon be evident in the chapters to come, the separation-individuation themes may become encapsulated repetitions with minimal variation, burying the Real Self, metaphorically.

Before a very synoptic psychoanalytic rendering of Masterson's Mahler is attempted, it is of importance to turn to Mahler herself concerning the developmental stages evident in separation-individuation when she writes,

> Neither the normal autistic, the normal symbiotic, not any subphase of separation-individuation is *completely replaced* by the subsequent phase. From a descriptive point of view, it is possible to see similarities among them: they can be conceptually differentiated on the basis of clusters of behavioral phenomena, but they overlap considerably.
>
> (Mahler et al., 1975, p. 48)

Although the phases will be written essentially linearly, clinical psychoanalysis teaches that developmental opportunities, demands, and conflicts are ever-present, and the developmental self and object relations psychoanalyst's ear will be attuned to the *rhythms* inherent in separation-individuation. Also, as many may view Mahler as outdated, much of Mahlerian thinking has greatly supported contemporary models such as the highly detailed *Developmental Structuralist Psychoanalytic Model* (DSPM)[5] that follows a meticulous ego-psychological perspective.[6] Space, unfortunately, prohibits a more complex and nuanced exposition of the growth of Mahlerian thinking. To understand Masterson's rich conceptualizations, Mahler's original thinking pertaining to developmental psychoanalysis and object relations will be discussed under the following headings:

Autism: 0–2 months
Symbiosis: 2–6 months
Separation-individuation: 6–24 months

- Hatching subphase: 6–10 months
- Practicing subphase: 10–16 months
- Rapprochement subphase: 16–24 months

Developing Object Constancy: 24–36+ months

The Normal Autistic Phase: Birth–Two Months – The Psyche as Dali's Egg

Despite contemporary psychoanalytic debates[7,8] concerning an autistic phase of development (i.e., Donald Stern[9] and his thinking on the clinical infant versus the observed infant), early Mahler, primarily influenced by Freud's egg model, held that the infant's perceptual system enters the world encapsulated. Due to a highly sensitive and underdeveloped nervous system (although imbued with immense growth capacity), a protective "hardened" although porous "shell" with all its nutrients available for further growth serves as an envelope to the infant's[10] psyche. Earlier psychoanalytic thinkers thus held that the primordial I or self remains enveloped and perceptually "limited" in recognizing the other as other in the autistic phase. Surrealist painter Salvador Dali's[11] work personifies such a view, and many encapsulated pathologies, from sensory sensitivity (autism) to bodily encapsulation (anorexia) to thinking-feeling encapsulation of mind (delusional states, claustra) reflect the egg metaphor, although clearly on different levels of representation and complexity. Anni Bergman (1999) also writes that Mahler later agreed that a normal autistic phase might not be possible as she conceptualized earlier. However, some of Mahler's intuitive descriptions have stood the test of time and have been used by various psychoanalysts, notably Francis Tustin and Judith Mitrani. Mahler did hold that in the autistic phase, the infant has to achieve some sort of physiological homeostasis, the inner physiological world becoming synchronized with the vocal and gestural rhythms of the mothering other. Even in utero, the infant is an active partner when considering the concept of mother-fetal microchimerism. Distal and proximal coordination remain physiological, physical, and "intra"–"inter" "regional" vertices able to organize all later psychological development. Connected and separated by the umbilicus, connected inside mom from the outside, by birth, separated yet connected through biological and psychological imperatives. Connection, separation-growth, and individuation are *indelibly* imprinted processes throughout all subsequent human development.

In the normal autistic phase, there seems, thus, despite an explicit partnering of the mother other, a limited cathexis of external stimuli. Following Freud's concept of primary narcissism (1914) and Ferenczi's (1913, in Mahler et al., 1975) stage of absolute hallucinatory omnipotence, the first few weeks of extrauterine life find the infant *lacking an awareness* of a mothering object. Despite the latter, and in rapid succession in development, reflex equipment such as sucking, rooting, and clinging as a "primitive coenesthetic transaction" (Mahler et al., 1975, p. 43) turns to visual following. Hartman (1939, in Mahler et al., 1975) held that the child enters the world of others with the necessary psychological equipment for *primary autonomy* and that in the autistic phase, the equipment follows the "rules of the coenesthetic organization of the central nervous system; the reaction to any stimulus that surpasses the threshold of reception in the weeks of normal autism is global, diffuse, syncretic-reminiscent of fetal life" (Mahler et al., 1975, p. 43). Early Mahler also mentions that external stimuli, although not cathected as in later stages of development mainly due to perceptual immaturity, do find the one-month-old responsive, described as "alert inactivity." Infants respond to light, movement, sound, taste, touch, warmth, cold, and smell, although they seem unable to differentiate between human and non-human stimuli. For Hamilton, in a more or less closed psychological system, the newborn is initially cloaked in "the reverie of a sleeplike state. The newborn's psychological withdrawal approximates the insulation of intrauterine life. Such an oblivion provides an intermediary zone between intrauterine and extrauterine life" (1988, p. 36). Guntrip adds an object relations dimension when he writes:

> The mother first supplies the baby with his basis for 'being' while he is still in the womb,[12] and must be able to prolong that secure experience of 'being-at-one-with-her' after birth, so that as the baby begins to experience his physical and psychological separateness

> from the mother on a conscious level, he is protected, by the unconscious persistence of the feeling of '*being-one-with,*' from the shock of what might be otherwise be experienced as a feeling of being 'cut off,' lost, dying.[13] A secure sense of being, shared with a stable mother before and after birth, must remain as a permanent foundation in the unconscious, on the basis of which a separate ego-identity can develop stably and elaborate into a highly individual personality.
>
> (Guntrip, 1969, p. 266) (italics added)

Hamilton also mentions, in homage to Guntrip, that the reason adults may find it difficult to conceptualize an autistic phase is that they attach to their infants in the most profound ways. Holding a newborn evokes a deep oneness with new life – it can be argued that adults enter a partial fusional state with newborns and are emotionally and psychologically invested in the newborn, projecting the psychological soil from which the matrix of self and other will emerge. It is also frightening to envision a catastrophic lack of a caring and holding other to support the infant's gradual orientation to the world.

The Normal Symbiotic Phase: One–Five Months

Symbiosis, given Mahler and other's work, should be read as a *metaphor*;

> It describes that stage of undifferentiation, of fusion with mother, in which the "I" is not yet differentiated from the "not I" and which inside and outside are only gradually coming to be sensed as different…The essential feature of symbiosis is hallucinatory or delusional somatopsychic omnipotent fusion with the representation of the mother and, in particular, the delusion of a common boundary between two physically separate individuals.
>
> (Mahler et al., 1975, pp. 44–45)

Given total dependence on the mother, she is tasked to protect the infant's rudimentary ego from overstimulation and premature phase specific strain and stress traumata. Mothering here can be viewed as "a kind of *social symbiosis*" (Mahler et al., 1975, p. 45), and the social symbiosis serves as the foundation for a functioning ego over time. As previously written (Daws, 2009), connection and separation are negotiated even in these earlier phases of development: full body holding, breast in the oral cavity (fusion), and eye-to-eye contact (distal/separation) with a communicative mother. In Henry Elkin's (1958, 1972) and Michael Eigen's (1986) genius, the body ego (holding and mouth) and the transcendental ego (T-ego, eye-to-eye) are thus formed. Without too much detail, for Elkin, the transcendental ego (eye-to-eye) predates the body ego as the first and foremost ego. Such differentiation, combined with the fusional capacity and hallucinatory and delusional qualities, may serve as the reason for not only symbiotic child psychosis but even the dreamworlds of the psychotic, severe eating disorders, schizoaffective disorders, and regressive schizoid states of mind. These regions of being may remain accessible to the exceedingly creative individual and our most receptive psychoanalysts such as Harry Stack Sullivan, Harold Searles, Margaret Little, Masud Khan, C.G. Jung, Michael Eigen, and many others.

During social symbiosis (the *dawning awareness* of a two-person psychology), a dual development occurs. The tenderness of the mothering one supports the gathering of experience and a further maturing of the central nervous system. Through such tender holding, the infant increasingly develops a dim awareness of this need-satisfying part object and begins to behave as if the mothering one is part of the omnipotent self-system, that is, "within the orbit of the omnipotent *symbiotic dual unity*" (Mahler et al., 1975, p. 46). Given such growing awareness and dual unity, the rudimentary ego (self) becomes increasingly capable of mediating between inner and outer perceptions, and "from the standpoint of the body image, the shift of predominantly proprioceptive-interoceptive cathexis toward *sensoriperceptive cathexis of the periphery* is a major step in development" (Mahler et al., 1975, p. 46) (italics added). The development of the rudimentary body ego and the shift of cathexis from exclusively proprioceptive-interoceptive cathexis toward sensoriperceptive experience is of great importance as the infant's inner sensations form the *core* of the self. They remain the central crystallization point of the "feeling of self" around which a "sense of identity" will become established. The sensoriperceptive organ – the "peripheral rind of the ego," as Freud called it – also contributes to the self's *differentiation*/demarcation from the outer world. The two kinds of intrapsychic structure *together* form the framework for self-orientation. A patient reflected as follows:

> As I feel my feelings, rather feel the sensations in me, I think...O! That is hunger, I am hungry – *I* am hungry! Then I feel fear...it is too much. I touch my stomach, try to be aware, and only now do I start to remember what an issue food was in our house – between my mom and I. My mom's reactions when I was hungry, *her mood changing my tummy, my hunger, changing me*! I forgot all of this... repressed? Obliviate! Her need became mine? Mine hers?

Within the symbiotic orbit, the two partners may be regarded as creatively valorizing and polarizing the organizational and structuring processes (self and other). The structures that derive from this double frame of reference (dual union) represent a framework to which all experiences must be related before there are explicit and whole representations in the ego of the self and the object world. Spitz (1965, in Mahler et al., 1975) calls the mother the auxiliary ego of the infant. Similarly, we believe the mothering partner's "holding behavior," her "primary maternal preoccupation" in Winnicott's sense (1958), functions as the symbiotic organizer – the midwife of individuation, of *psychological birth* (Mahler et al., 1975).

Furthermore, the normal symbiotic phase marks the all-important phylogenetic capacity of the human infant to psychologically invest the mothering other *within* a vague dual unity,[14] effectively forming the primal soil from which all subsequent human relationships will develop (Eigen, 1986). Given the primordial psychophysiological self's[15] inborn autonomous perceptive capacities and need for ego-relatedness, Mahler accentuates the primordial accumulation of the pleasure-displeasure self-object interaction and its memory traces, forming the psychic foundation "of the two primordial qualities of stimuli [that] occur within the primal undifferentiated matrix" (Mahler et al., 1975, p. 44). Hamilton writes that this ever-increasing accumulation of memory traces of that which is unpleasurable (bad) stands in contrast with that which is pleasurable (good), increasingly defining the "budding 'self-and-object images' during the symbiotic phase of development and thereafter. Pleasure and pain, good and bad, become a second polarity around which the child organizes its world, along with the self-other polarity" (1988, p. 40).

With good enough mothering and holding, the smiling response heralds the symbiotic relationship. As many have written, the smiling response is one of the first signs of a genuine relationship (i.e., ego-relatedness), of tenderness evoked and responded to, of mutual cuing being productive. Parents usually experience joy, delight, and closeness in the symbiotic stage. Developmental difficulties may subdue the pleasure symbiosis may bring, and I will return to this difficulty in Chapter 4. Furthermore, it is essential to clinically keep in mind that the oceanic feeling of oneness and the reality of dual union finds an infantile mind "experiencing," "thinking," and "feeling" in a particular fashion (poor self-other differentiation). That is, when the infant moves his head or eyes, the mother magically appears! When the infant moves, so the world moves, "Omnipotence permeates the baby's symbiotic world. As the baby moves, the world moves; as the baby feels, the world feels; as the baby breathes, the world breathes" (Hamilton, 1988, p. 40).

Separation-Individuation (6–24 months)

Subphase One: Differentiation – 5–10 Months

The movement from intramural to extramural life to a growing awareness of the mothering half of his symbiotic self is especially evident in the smiling response, a sign of a genuine bond. Safe and secure anchorage, molding the body to the mothering other, also sees the reality of "hatching," the tentative use of transitional objects in the transitional situation, checking back patterns (seven–eight months), and stranger reactions and anxiety. The hatching process can be seen as "the gradual ontogenetic evolution of the sensorium – the perceptual-conscious system – which enables the infant to have a more permanently alert sensorium whenever he is awake" (Mahler et al., 1975, p. 53). Mahler mentions that this awakening and attention is a matter of degree rather than kind, although there is now a "new look of alertness, persistence, and goal-directedness" (p. 54). The mother's comings and goings, her affective attunement, and the quality of the affective exchange between mother and child are stored as memory islands of pleasure and displeasure, further supporting the structuralization of good and bad self-other feelings. Given a greater awakening at six months, the first tentative experimentation with separation and individuation becomes increasingly evident. Molding (symbiosis) is replaced by pushing away (distancing) from the mother to get a better look at the mother, especially her face, introducing the concept of "customs inspection." Customs inspection is broadened by activities such as putting food in the mother's mouth and other exploration patterns, supporting mother-not-mother differentiation.

Mahler reminds us in her writing that this is also the stage where transitional objects and situations, a la Winnicott, occur, and disturbances here serve as the first sign of possible psychotic disturbance and later borderline conditions. *Checking back at the mother* furthers developmental evidence of somatopsychic differentiation and sees the growing reliance on comparative scanning to aid separation-differentiation; that is, the mother is actively compared to, and thus differentiated from, the environment aiding cognitive-perceptual development; "He seems to familiarize himself more thoroughly, as it were, with what *is* mother, what feels, tastes, smell, looks like, and has the '*clang*' of mother" (Mahler et al., 1975, p. 56). By definition, such familiarization, differentiation, and separation bring further affective realities, as mentioned, in the form of *stranger anxiety*. If the mother's face and body were mainly experienced as *a basis of pleasure and trust,* stranger anxiety could be tolerated and used for further differentiation of not-mother. The infant is then set to turn in "confident expectation" (Mahler et al., 1975, p. 57) toward the work of differentiation (the not-mother) with wonderment and curiosity.

Transient anxiety may indeed interfere with pleasurable inspective behavior, which is needed for further separation-individuation. If the symbiotic stage, characterized by the shielding membrane of the dual unity, has been delayed or disturbed, the infant may be subject to various developmental adaptations that may inhibit, if not thwart, its natural hatching capacities. The psyche's adaptations may vary, given the types of mothering the infant was exposed to. For example, relating to a mother struggling with post-partum psychosis may differ from the affective indifference of a depressed mother. Adaptation could include autoerotic preferences such as taking the body as object, combined with an undifferentiated smile response (to external objects), to a delayed use of mother as a vitalizing other affecting somatopsychic differentiation, especially in the visual field (distance perceptual). Compensatory structures can also find precocious ego development,[16] that is, precocious hatching, a "knowing" based on managing the environment and mother, principally finding that the mother-child relationship improves when *distance is sought or held.* This pattern seems very reminiscent of Ferenczi's wise baby and the schizoid adaption a la, Fairbairn, Guntrip, and Masterson. Mahler writes that such premature ego development may serve as the basis of the "false self." Also, the presence of another object, such as a father, grandmother, etc., may protect a toddler by humanizing the world. Symbiotic enveloping and parasitic-like intrusiveness may see earlier distancing behaviors, especially if the mothering other prefers the passive molding quality of symbiosis. Mothers who cannot endure the gradual disengagement may

> attach, appersonate, the infant to themselves and discourage his groping for independent functioning, instead of allowing and promoting gradual separation. On the other hand…there is quite a large contingent of mothers who, unlike the overly symbiotic mothers, at first hold onto their infants and then push him precipitously into autonomy.
>
> (Mahler et al., 1975, pp. 62–63)

However, as the dyad adapts to "a to-and-fro movement of closeness and distance – the dance of separation-individuation – has begun" (Hamilton, 1988, p. 43).

Subphase Two: Practicing – 10–16 Months

The practicing subphase can be differentiated into two parts – an early practicing subphase characterized by growing motility such as crawling, climbing, etc., while still holding on to the practicing period proper, characterized by free upright locomotion. This period finds more significant differentiation from the mothering other, rapid body differentiation, and growth of the autonomous ego apparatus. The infant gradually turns to the world of inanimate objects for exploration, comfort, and self-other articulation (transitional objects). As mentioned in the previous section, significant locomotion and the use of distance may serve some mother-child relationships wherein the dual unity was experienced as unsatisfactory, contrasting sharply with those who enjoyed the symbiosis but prefer to have their children all grown up by its end. Mahler found the children exposed to the latter attitude struggling with distance and demanded closeness. This stands in contrast with locomotion in service of exploring the world – negotiating the "coming-and-going" with mother, every step growing in autonomy while seeking maternal warmth and kindness as needed. How the world is experienced is significantly colored by the way in which the mother supports his interest and movement. The *mother of symbiosis* subtly shifts to the *mother of separation.* Mother-infant reunion and separation build the fragile although ever-expanding inner world of the human infant. Returning to object relations theory, given the largest of the caretaking others, and in accordance with the psychoanalytic theories of both Elkin (1958, 1972) and Eigen (1986, 1999), the intensity of inner affect storms and experiences, as well as the fragility of self-other representations and its ego defenses, the *representations of self and others* here may be more accurately referred to as the *divine self* in relation to the *heavenly mother* and/or the *evil or diabolical mother,* instead of the good or bad mother. Such an image is frequently represented through art, i.e., the Great or Divine Mother and Divine Child. Such a description would also align with H.S. Sullivan (1953) and many others on the good, bad, and *evil nipple*. It is not infrequent to find, somewhat in unison with the latter, infants described as "angelic" or "a little devil." Despite the growing capacity to enjoy the mother over a distance and the necessary investment of libido in the toddler's autonomous functions, the mother remains "home base," an anchor to return to for emotional refueling.

With the practicing subphase proper, Mahler further conceptualized a toddler caught up in a *love affair* with the world, given their upright locomotion. With a more significant narcissistic investment in the body ego and its ever-expanding capacities, the toddler seems relatively impervious to knocks, falls, and limits; the *natural world's values of cause-and-effect* unable to dim the expansive feel and love affair with both the bodily and mental self-and-world. Not only is narcissism at its peak but it is held that some of the elation experienced may be attributed to the *growing* separation from the fusion (if not engulfment) with the mother, evident in the play between mother and toddler. Peek-a-boo, turning passive into active, finds the toddler experiencing delight in partaking in the various games of catch-and-release. It is important to note that Mahler conceptualizes that this playful catch-and-release reassures the growing toddler that the mothering other still *wants* to connect with him. Mother's presence, attitude, and gentle support play a pivotal role in the experience of upright locomotion. Mother's absence in this stage also sees the presence of low-keyedness. The latter can be described as an inwardly concentrated attention termed "imaging," reflecting a particular "state of self." More specifically, it may indicate that the toddler remains susceptible to losing an "ideal state of self," and the low-keyedness, given the mother's absence and thus the elation of reunion, may reflect a *miniature anaclitic depression.* Mahler poignantly writes on toddlers' increased awareness that the symbiotic mothering half of the self may be lost, missed, or experienced as absent (void experiences).

Subphase Three: Rapprochement – 16–24 Months

As beautifully written by Mahler, the attainment of upright locomotion, as well as the attainment of a stage of cognitive development Piaget would regard as the beginning of representational intelligence (to culminate in speech and capacity for symbolic play), "the human being has emerged as a separate autonomous person. These two powerful 'organizers' constitute the midwives of psychological birth" (Mahler et al., 1975, p. 76). As a toddler, the child makes greater use of his physical separateness, scaffolding significant cognitive and emotional differentiation. However, considerable separation anxiety is observed due to the waning of imperviousness and obliviousness to the mother's presence and absence (due to intrapsychic symbiosis). That is, the mother's emotional availability and sensitivity to the separation-anxious toddler in rapprochement is of immense developmental importance,

> One cannot emphasize too strongly the importance of the optimally emotional availability of the mother during this subphase. It is the mother's love of the toddler and the acceptance of his ambivalence that enable the toddler to cathect his self-representation with neutralized energy.
>
> (Mahler et al., 1975, p. 77)

Mahler further differentiated *rapprochement* into three periods: (a) the beginning rapprochement; (2) the rapprochement crisis; and (3) variable individual "solutions" and "adaptations" to this crisis, all resulting in a "patterning and *personality characteristics* with which the child enters into the fourth subphase of separation-individuation, the consolidation of individuation" (Mahler et al., 1975, p. 89). In the beginning rapprochement period, increased separation anxiety finds the toddler shadowing and darting as a way to communicate both the wish for reunion and fear of engulfment (especially if the mother herself shadows the child due to her own symbiotic needs). The mother is also responsible for sustaining constructive (neutralized) aggression to further the emerging self. In the rapprochement crisis, greater *ambitendency*[17] is observed (18–24 months), indicative of the painful struggle of approach-avoidance,[18] i.e., the various attempts to push the mother away alternating with both approaching and clinging to the mother. During the earlier phases, the *mother is used as an extension of the toddler's self*, denying the painful awareness of her separateness. The powerful impact of differentiation and awareness of the mother's protection also finds a resurgence of *stranger reactions*, even toward people to whom the toddler previously responded positively. *Indecision* can also be found in this development period, concretely represented as standing on the *threshold* between two worlds. For Mahler, indecision "would seem to be the perfect symbolization of conflicting wishes – the wish to enter the toddler world away from mother and the pull to remain with mother in the infant room" (Mahler et al., 1975, p. 96). During this phase, cognitively, the toddler seems able to achieve some object permanence, knowing the mother could be elsewhere and found. Despite this achievement, being left alone for too long significantly impacts the growing toddler – lowering mood and the ability to play. Combined with the cumulative good-enough experiences of the previous stages, the growing child can progressively work on the good and bad mother representations – with the hope the holding environment ensures integration and ambivalence with time. As will be evident in the chapters to come, and considering the pre-Oedipal nature of the disorders of self, maternal over and/or under-stimulation finds the child, and later adult, reliant on *split* self and object representations lacking in integration. Mahler's team found many different degrees and variations concerning splitting, although for most toddlers protecting a good internal mother finds the projection of the bad mother onto the environment, acting angry at the separation.

Subphase Four: Consolidation and Object Constancy – 24–36 Months

For Mahler, the main task of the fourth subphase is as follows: "(1) the achievement of a definite, in certain aspects *lifelong, individuality*, and (2) the attainment of *a degree* of object constancy" (Mahler et al., 1975, p. 109) (italics added). The achievement of affective object constancy is based on the gradual and progressive internalization of a positively cathected internal image of the mother. The constancy of the object is based not only on the maintenance of the good object representation in its absence but also on the unification of both the good and bad representation into a whole object representation intrapsychically. The process is long and complex and is based on the (a) neutralization of aggression, (b) the maintenance of basic trust in the mother of symbiosis and of separation-individuation, (c) the child's cognitive maturation enabling representational development needed for symbolic inner representation of the permanent object (a la Piaget), (d) the child's innate drive endowment, (e) capacity for reality testing based on an intact perceptual system, and an "acceptable" (f) window of tolerance for anxiety and frustration (and much more). Object constancy, itself a growing capacity, allows for more extraordinary lengths of parental absences as the child manages the various transitions of development with and without the mothering other. Cognitive growth is also scaffolded by verbal communication, fantasy (fantasy play, role-playing, make-believe), and, more significantly, more significant reality testing. It is believed that through the growing capacity to separate and individuate, the "Real Self" will gradually come into being, although the other remains a vital and necessary partner throughout all development. Mahler adds that no less than six factors may determine the outcome of the rapprochement crisis: (a) the achievement, over time, of libidinal object constancy, (b) the exposure to shock trauma, (c) the degree of castration anxiety, (d) both the quantity and quality of disappointments or stress trauma, (e) the resolution of the Oedipus complex, and (f) the developmental crisis of adolescence as the second phase of coming up against the object of frustration.

The Mother's Role in the Genesis and Psychic Structure of the Disorder of Self Analysands

Reading developmental psychoanalysis and object relations theorists such as Masterson and others, the clinician may appreciate that the mother of symbiosis, separation-individuation, and the Oedipal phase (and beyond), calls forth different attitudes and functions. The mother-child interaction remains complex, although it can tentatively be argued that the presence of stereotyped repetitions of maladaptive themes (non-verbal and verbal) may give rise to intrapsychic and developmental phenomena observable in the transference and therapeutic acting out, serving as a clue to separation-individuation difficulties. Given the current state of research, it may be argued, especially reviewing the work of Masterson's early colleague, Donald Rinsley

(1982),[19] that severe maternal misperception (psychotic variation) of the child may be reflected in relating to the child as an inanimate object (a doll, toy, and such), as part of one's own body and its functions (symbolic representations of the parent's eyes, excretions, etc.), as subhuman, monstrous, nonexistent, or abolished.[20] Concerning less severe misattunement, i.e., borderline and narcissistic patterning, Rinsley (1982) notes that the child may be perceived as a surrogate parental figure, ensuring a role reversal. The child becomes a superego representation providing guidance, controls, and limits for the parent. The child can also be perceived as a spouse, creating an overt or covert incestuous relationship, or a sibling, stimulating rather destructive patterns of competition and rivalry. Finally, the child can also be misperceived as an "endlessly infantile or dependent baby" (1982, p. 202), mainly reflecting the parent's need to keep the child from growing up and having a life of its own. The following chapters will pay detailed attention to the variation and patterning as reflected in Masterson's split object relations units.

The Role of the Father in Normal Separation-Individuation

Whereas it can be argued that the infant must separate and differentiate *from* the symbiotic dual unity with the mother, the father's representation[21] comes from *without*, i.e., *toward* the child. Although the father can be involved in the symbiotic phase proper, his presence becomes essential as a partner in separation-individuation and the Oedipal stage *with* the mother. Masterson agrees with this understanding and cites Abelin's research on the role of the father in the separation-individuation process;

> For fathers involved with their infants, although not as early as for the mother, a relationship with father is possible as early as the symbiotic phase, countering stranger anxiety towards him. During the differentiation suphase, the *practicing suphase father* can become the exciting and different other towards which the child can turn. Mother as home base, given the intrapsychic fusion may be taken for granted! The father comes to stand for distant, "non-mother" space—for the elated exploration of reality. A special quality of exuberance is linked with him.
>
> (Abelin, in Masterson, 1981, p. 12) (italics added)

Even more powerfully written, Masterson (1981, p. 14) proposes,

> We might summarize the father's contribution to normal ego development in the separation-individuation phase of development as follows: 1. to serve as an object uncontaminated with symbiotic cathexis, to draw and attract a child into the real world of things and people; 2. in the rapprochement subphase to serve as a parental love object which aligns itself with reality and the forces of individuation as opposed to the regressive pull toward the mother and therefore to contribute to the successful resolution of the rapprochement phase; and 3. to participate in the construction of mental images of the self, the maternal object and the paternal object—the *forerunner to the oedipal complex.*[22]
>
> (Italics added)

In all treatments of the disorders of the self, both the maternal and the paternal object become part of the separation-individuation process and its vicissitudes. Both parents may collude in using the child as a scapegoat, triangulate the child, or act out their own separation-individuation conflicts. Masterson also explores in various volumes the complexity when the identification with the father serves as a defense against the mother, necessitating more challenging working through cycles (see especially Masterson, 1976).

Notes

1 For an in-depth discussion also see Orcutt, 1989, Chapter 7, as well as her book *The Unanswered Self* published in 2021 for detailed debates on Masterson's concepts as they relate, integrate, and diverge from other developmental psychoanalysts.

2 From the psychoanalytic mind and pen of Christopher Bollas: "Our internal world is transformed by the mother's unconscious desire into a primary theme of being with her that will affect all future ways of being with the other" and "We have internalized a process, a forming and transforming idiom, as well as the thematics of mother's discourse. Whenever we desired, despaired, reached towards, played, or were in rage, love, pain or need, we were met by mother and handled according to her idiom of care. Whatever our existential critique of her aesthetic, be it generative integration into our own being, compliance followed by dissociated splitting of our true self, or defensive handling of the aesthetic (denial, splitting, repression) we encountered her idiom. Indeed, the way she handled us (either as accepting and facilitating or refusing and rigid or a mixture of

both) will influence our way of handling our self. *In a sense, we learn the grammar of our being before we grasp the rules of our language*" (1986, pp. 35–36) (italics added).

3 Although both Masterson and Winnicott use the term "False Self," there are clear conceptual and clinical differences. The reader is also referred to Masterson's 1976 and 2004 work for clarification.

4 Sensationally: part of body-ego experiences, taste, touch, smell, sound, sight, referring to the materiality of the object.

   Structurally: referring to the objects' "atomic specificity" and specific use-potential. When used, it creates experiences true to its use-potential. For example, the difference between using a jumping rope and playing golf.

   Conceptually and symbolically: objects have names and are part of a symbolic order.

   Mnemically: objects can also be endowed with previous self-experiences.

   Protectively: particular objects can be used to contain parts of our self-experiences as to be re-experienced, elaborated, etc.; for example, in reading a book, I might be reworking a voyeuristic part of self.

5 Please see the table entitled *Human Development: Birth to Three Years* in Chatham, 1985, pp. 204–205, as well as the table *Stages of Ego Development* in Greenspan, 1989, pp. 64–66.

6 The DSPM enables the modern clinician in tracking the development of *self and object representation* as seen through the five phases of separation-individuation as described by Colarusso (2000). It includes the *nuclear self* and the pre-caesura reality, somatic pre-intentional world self-object, intentional part self-object, differentiated behavioral part self-object, functional (conceptual) integrated and differentiated self-object, representational self-object elaboration, and differentiated-integrated representational self-object:

   (1) The *nuclear self* and pre-caesura mentality serve as the first psychic organizer and are described in great detail by Roy Mendelsohn (1987a, 1987b, 1987c, 1987d) and David and Jill Scharff (1991, pp. 22–23) as the psychological movement from the pre-birth somatic partnership to the establishment of a psychosomatic (symbiotic) partnership at birth.
   (2) *Homeostasis,* which includes self-regulation and interest in the world, and spans the first three months of development.
   (3) The *attachment phase,* which is evident between the second and seventh months of development.
   (4) The phase of *somato-psychological differentiation*, which includes purposeful communication and is observable between the third and tenth month of development.
   (5) The phase of *behavioral organization, initiative, and internalization* that serves as the foundation for a *complex sense of self.* This stage usually develops between the ninth and eighteenth months of development.

(6) The *representational capacity or symbolic* phase, which is evident between 18 and 30 months of development.
(7) The *representational differentiation* phase, which emerges between the second and fourth years of life.
(8) These phases (2–7) are based on Mahler's initial developmental phases and subphases of development.

7 Gotstein's description, "Tustin (1980, 1981a,b) formulates that there are two major kinds of psychotic children, the encapsulated type (infantile autistic psychosis proper) and the confusional type (childhood schizophrenia). Both types suffer from premature psychological birth, at-one-ment from the bonding object with the resultant precipitation of a premature 'two-ness.' These hapless children seem not to have a transitional bridge to the object and consequently become "autosensual," by which Tustin means that the infant's senses, which are normally the bridge to the object, no longer extend to the object, who is now experienced as being dangerously far away and alien" (1986, p. 97).
8 Also see works such as J. Mario Gomberoff, C. Carmen Noemi, L. Pualuan de Gomberoff, 1990, *The Autistic Object: Its Relationship With Narcissism in the Transference and Countertransference of Neurotic and Borderline Patients,* published in the *Int J Psychoanal*, 71 (2), 249–259.
9 In Orcutt's writing (2021, pp. 109–110): "However, in the exchange between them noted by Stern, Mahler herself had second thoughts about her use of terms so absolute and suggestive of pathology: 'In a recent discussion, she suggested that this initial phase might well have been called 'awakening,' which is very close to 'emergence' as it has been called here [Mahler, personal communication 1983]' (Stern, 1985, p. 235)."
10 Tustin, F. (1981/2013). Psychological birth and psychological catastrophe. In *Autistic States in Children* (pp. 96–110). New York: Routledge.
11 I am reminded here of Dali's *Geopoliticus Child Watching the Birth of the New Man*, 1943.
12 I previously referred to this phenomenon as pre-Caesura reality (2009).
13 The work of Michael Eigen refers, in my understanding, to the latter as deficits in the "Embryonic Self" (1998, p. 99).
14 As mentioned, the visual representations as created by David and Jill Scharff (1991, pp. 22–23) on the pre-birth somatic partnership to the establishment of a psychosomatic (symbiotic) partnership at birth remains invaluable in reading Mahler.
15 Term used by other psychoanalysts such as Edith Jacobson, Otto Fenichel, H. Hartmann, R.M. Loewenstein, and E. Kris.
16 Please see Christopher Fortune's article *The Analytic Nursery: Ferenczi's "Wise Baby" Meets Jung's "Divine Child"* published in the Journal of Analytic Psychology, 2003, 48, pp. 457–466. I will discuss in Chapter 4 onwards the importance of the symbiotic phase of development and the presence of the *Divine Child* (the domain of "psychosis") as related to hatching pathology, the schizoid process, and the *Wise Child.*
17 As defined by Mahler et al., "The simultaneous presence of two contrasting, behaviorally manifest tendencies; for example, the child may cry and smile virtually at the same time, approach mother and the last moment veer

away, or kiss mother and suddenly bite her. Ambitendency is behaviourally biphasic; it may or may not soon be replaced by ambivalence, where the biphasic tendency is integrated and no longer observable" (1975, p. 289).

18 Those struggling within the borderline dilemma are frequently misunderstood as being ambivalent rather than struggling with ambitendency toward their love objects. Ambivalence remains a developmental achievement!

19 Also see the work of Christine Ann Lawson (2000) entitled, *Understanding the Borderline Mother – Helping her Children Transcend the Intense, Unpredictable, Volatile Relationship*, wherein she discusses various kinds of mothers; (a) the make-believe mothers, (b) the waif-mother, (c) the hermit-mother, (d) the Queen-mother, (e) the witch-mother, as well as fairy tale fathers.

20 For Rinsley, "Characteristics of some postpartum psychotic mothers, this extreme pattern involves a scotomatization or negative hallucination of the newborn child which may extend into later childhood" (1982, p. 202).

21 For an in-depth read and discussion on the father's role in SI, please see Masterson, 1981, pp. 11–14, and 22.

22 "The symbolic representation of the father must be distinguished from the actual relationship with him. The rapprochement crisis is at first centered solely on the representation of the self and the mother. A few weeks later, the father begins to appear in the fantasy world of the toddler as the other, more powerful parent. *This father image may be necessary for the satisfactory resolution of the ambivalent rapprochement position.* The simultaneous representation of the three images of the self and both parents would constitute an even more elaborate step—perhaps representing the formal element of the oedipal complex. Thus, the development of these nuclear images after the rapprochement subphase would seem to recapitulate the earlier history of the actual specific relationship—in a distilled and schematized form. In cognitive development, Piaget (105) has called this recapitulation a 'vertical lag'" (Masterson, 1981, p. 13).

Chapter 3

Key Concepts in the Developmental Self and Object Relations Approach of James Masterson

Introduction

For the Masterson approach, various organizing principles support the developmental self and object relations approach to the disorder of self analysand. That is, this chapter will emphasize concepts such as the (Real) Self, the ego, and the False Self, the impact of abandonment depression on general development and the disorders of self triads, the importance of therapeutic neutrality in containing transference acting out, and the use of communicative matching and countertransference in the general treatment of the disorders of self.

The Self, Ego, Real and False Self

According to Masterson (2004, p. 16), the self and ego can be defined as follows:

> The self and the ego develop and function *in parallel*; for example, like two horses in tandem in the same harness. The self is the representational arm of the ego, and the ego is the executive arm of the self, although each is more than that. If the ego is arrested developmentally, the self will also be arrested developmentally... The self, of course, is mostly preconscious and conscious; through its synthesizing functions, the ego is mostly unconscious. *The ego's synthesizing function does for the psyche what respiration and circulation do for the soma.*
>
> (italics added)

DOI: 10.4324/9781003358572-4

Masterson further defines the "Real Self"[1] as consisting of the sum total of the intrapsychic images of the self with its associated object representations. Furthermore, the term "Real" implies an adaptive and flexible self able to support various functions that will soon be discussed, i.e., self-activation, having a sense of agency, soothing painful affects, and much more. For Masterson, the Real Self contains two main functions: "it provides the emotional vehicle for self-expression, and it also operates to maintain self-esteem through the mastery of reality tasks" (Masterson et al., 2004, p. 14). In contrast with the Real Self, the False Self[2] aims at protecting the impaired self from developmental and relational pain at the expense of further separation-individuation. The senior Mastersonian Dr. Don Roberts provides the following poignant description concerning the reality of a False Self,

> There is the self we are born with, and then of course the world does its work...The world sets into making us into what the world would like us to be, and because we have to survive after all, we try to make our selves into something that we hope the world will like better than it apparently did the selves we originally were. That is the story of all our lives, needless to say, and in the process of living out that story, the original, shimmering self gets buried so deep that most of us end up hardly living out of it at all.
>
> (Buechner, 1991, p. 45, in Roberts and Roberts, 2007, p. 44)

The Real Self is dependent on the separation of internalized self-representations from internalized object representations through separation-individuation. During separation-individuation, the internalized object representations are hoped to reflect supportive and life-giving qualities, joyfully fueling (and refueling) the evolving self-representation's autochthonous adaptation. The child learns over time that their feelings, needs, and thoughts are distinct, separate, and acceptable by others. As described by many, this is not a given, and the child also seems unable to "know" that differences exist between "minds." The beginning of life thus finds a lack of distinction between self and others. The child feels and thinks of herself and her mother as a dual unity – a single cognitive, affective, and physical unit (Mahler et al., 1975). Mahler writes on *internal symbiosis*; Stern refers to this as the child's theory of *one-mindedness*; and for Masterson, the developmental state of *like-mindedness*. Internal symbiosis must evolve to include the mental capacity to hold a "theory" (a consensually validated view) of "separate but interfaceable minds" able to tolerate the integration of contradictory and opposite affect states. In early development, the toddler relies mainly on splitting to separate contradictory affect states with its self and object representations. That is, the good-me and good mommy with good feel is kept separate (*apart* to later "*a" part*) from bad me, bad mommy, and bad feelings. With evolving cognitive and affective development, the child begins to perceive self and others, thoughts, feelings, and behaviors as both containing good and bad (at the same time), neither wholly good nor bad, neither all white nor all black. The affective and cognitive growth also fuels the unfolding of various capacities of the "emerging" and "individuated" self. Through play, continual experimentation, adaptation, and supportive reinforcement from the good enough facilitating environment, Masterson's Real Self finds a child developing ontogenic *and* epistemological trust in the self and the other. The Real Self contrasts the False Self, a self that is mainly reactive, compliant, or hidden. For Masterson, the Real Self is evident in various characteristics:

- **Spontaneity and liveness of affect**: the capacity to experience affect deeply, freely, with liveliness, joy, vigor, and spontaneity.
- **Self-entitlement**: from the earliest experiences of self-body-world mastery coupled with supportive and loving parental acknowledgment for the emerging self, true confidence is born. This contact and growth teach the growing child that he or she is entitled to "appropriate experiences of mastery and pleasure, as well as to the environmental input necessary to achieve these objectives" (Klein, in Masterson et al., 1995, p. 6).
- **Self-activation, assertion, and support**: the capacity to identify one's unique wishes and take autonomous initiative through *assertive modes of being*. The latter also includes supporting and defending the self when negatively thwarted.
- **Acknowledgment of self-activation and maintenance of self-esteem**: to both identify and acknowledge to the self that one has coped with an affective state, an environmental demand, or a challenging self-state in an adaptive and transformative manner. Such an approach serves as the basis for maintaining self-esteem and positive self-regard.
- **The soothing of painful affects and the limiting of harmful cognitive scripts**: The capacity to autonomously regulate affects adequately, pleasurably, and in moderation as related to

environmental demands and interpersonal situations. Affects are also linked to evolving representations of self and others that may require seeking active support from others.

- **Continuity of self**: the conscious recognition and acknowledgment of an "I" over time and context.
- **Commitment**: the capacity to commit one's self to a relationship or objective and to persevere despite obstacles and setbacks.
- **Creativity or self-creation and its vicissitudes**: the ability to express the self in a way that strengthens trust in one's abilities as a unique once-in-a-lifetime being in the world. Being creative supports new psychological organizations fueled by the experience of ecstasy and transcendence. Ecstasy[3] supplies the Real Self with vitality affects, whereas transcendence finds the sharing of concepts of the world and from the world through our existentially informed self.
- **Intimacy**: the capacity to express the self in a relationship without fear of abandonment or engulfment.

In contrast to the Real Self, Masterson relies on the terms False Self (defensive self) and Impaired Self to accentuate its absence. As mentioned, the False Self is defined as a defensive structure that aims to protect the individual from immensely painful and frightening affects and memories, primarily due to the lack of support, adequate mirroring, misrecognition, strain, and cumulative trauma. The main aim of this "'defensive self" is not to deal with reality and maturation, but to *defend against mental pain and separation-individuation stress and trauma.* The *Impaired Self* can be defined as a deficit state

> that derives from a combined failure of nature, nurture, and fate to provide adequate support for the healthy development of the real self. The person with an impaired self lacks a sense that the self is adequate and worthy of support and compensates for that deficit with various defenses.
>
> (Klein, in Masterson et al., 1995, p. 53)

In Masterson's work, the principal motivating factor for the immense psychological pressure supporting the need for a false-self adaptation can be found in the reality of the painful unconscious abandonment depression.

Meeting Emily Dickenson's A Pain So Utter – Masterson's Abandonment Depression

Although nuanced and discussed in detail for all the disorders of self (see Chapters 4 onward), Masterson and Costello earliest formulations state (1980) that the natural surge of individuation in the child paradoxically induced withdrawal behavior from the mother, arresting the process of individuation, resulting in the experience of an abandonment depression, even more concerning, "Such depression can, on occasion, be recognized at the *age of three*. Whether or not it is apparent at age three, it will later emerge and become manifest during *adolescence*" (1980, p. 16, italics added). Masterson also writes that the abandonment depression should not be considered a single affect but reflects *six constituent emotions* (called the six psychiatric horsemen of the apocalypse) that include *depression*, *anger and rage*, *fear*, *guilt*, *passivity and helplessness*, *emptiness*, and *void*,

> These feeling states (listed above) vie in their emotional sway and destructiveness with the social upheaval and destructiveness of the original four horsemen: famine, war, flood and pestilence. *Technical words are too abstract to convey the intensity and immediacy of these feelings and, therefore, the primacy they hold over the patient's entire life.* The adolescent patient's functioning in the world, his relationships with people, and *even some of his physiologic functions are subordinated to the defense of these feelings.*
>
> (1980, p. 16) (italics added)

For Masterson, "The intensity and degree of each of these component feelings will vary with the unique developmental traumas of each individual. However, each component will be present to some degree in every patient" (1980, p. 16).

Depression

Depression, as found in pre-Oedipal patients (anaclitic-like), differs from reactive depressions or neurotic and guilt-driven depressions as they are experienced as threatening psychological survival;

> The depression has qualities similar to that feeling state described by Spitz as *anaclitic depression*: *feelings that spring from the loss*

> *or the threat of the loss either of part of the self or of supplies that the patient believes vital for survival.* Patients often report this in physical terms comparable to losing an arm or both legs, or being deprived of vital substances such as oxygen, plasma or blood.
>
> (1980, p. 17) (italics added)

During the *testing phase of therapy*, characterized by *transference acting out*, the analysand may only be vaguely aware of depressive feelings, most notably subtle feelings of anxiety, absence, and boredom. Holding the patient through the various approaches to be discussed in the following chapters, depressive affects are expected to become more intense, and if successful, may find the rise of painfully repressed memories linked with deprivation, loss, and abandonment. For Masterson, with deepening treatment, the analyst may also find a most painful belief that

> it will never be possible to receive the necessary supplies for living. At this point, the patient is a genuine suicidal risk, and there is no longer any doubt in the observer's mind about the motivational power of the patient's depression.
>
> (1980, p. 17)

An analysand responded in a session,

> I tried this week to say something to my husband, and then suddenly, I felt horribly frightened. Tasted bile, terrified. Sounds ridiculous, I know, but to speak is to lose…my whole life, to say what I really think would bring disaster…I do remember, from a young age…this feeling…vague memories of my mom getting so angry, her face, frightening…If I said, I don't want to or didn't like something…the anger. It is still in my body, like a cancer.

Rage

As the depression deepens, so too may one find the emergence of immense anger, rage, and even fury. The initial content of the rage may be ascribed to current external frustrations, but soon, the clinician will find, spontaneously, the emergence of maternal and paternal lack or engulfment. An analysand: "I have this immense anger, fury at how I comply with the needs of others and get fucked over. To be loved is to be fucked over; they don't care, don't care what I do for them, not even for myself. My husband can't stand being around me – critical of me and what I do. Not good enough ever...even my mother doesn't give a fuck about what I need. The voice in my head is criticizing me and putting me down ... I am hearing it in me and from my mother and husband – that I am useless, a nothing."

Fear and Panic

A third significant affect is the fear and panic of being abandoned. The fear and panic faced here are akin to *death anxiety*. Psychosomatic symptoms may even be observed in many patient experiences – introducing the claustrophobic-agoraphobic reality of the fear of engulfment, loss of the object, and being left helpless and vulnerable in a dangerous world. Masterson also found that

> The threat of abandonment apparently had been used as a disciplinary technique to inhibit the patient's self-assertion or expression of anger and to enforce compliance. Therefore, as the depression and rage emerge in psychotherapy, the fear of being abandoned for expressing these feelings rises in tandem, sometimes reaching panic proportions.
>
> (1980, p. 18)

A clinical example from Masterson may be helpful: A male analysand in his thirties spent years in treatment struggling with depression and his defensive self's destructive behavior, including drug use and promiscuity. As these symptomatic behaviors subsided, he reported,

> I had a *full-blown anxiety attack*—terrible dizziness. My fear of having this attack is what motivates that other self (*the defensive self*)—what used to keep me chasing alcohol, drugs, or women... If I take charge of myself (the real self), I will lose this notion of my mother. I would do anything to keep this image of her there. Alcohol, drugs, women. She never let me *grow up, I always* needed her close. I came to believe I couldn't function without her and I get overwhelmed with anxiety. It's hard to believe that at this age I could still have the feelings of an infant.
>
> (1985, p. 35)

Guilt

According to Masterson, guilt may be attributed to the introjection of the mother's anti-separation-individuation attitude, that is,

> Since the mother greeted the expression of his self-assertion and his wish to separate and individuate with disapproval and withdrawal, the patient begins to feel guilty about that whole part of himself which seeks separation and individuation; that is, *not only his actions but his thoughts, wishes and feelings*.
>
> (Masterson, 1980, pp. 18–19) (italics added)

The work of Dr. Judith Pearson adds another guilt dimension, that of survivor guilt; "I feel terrible to have a life, a life where my mom certainly had none. How can I allow myself a life of my own, knowing how much she struggles and has sacrificed for me?"

Passivity, Hopelessness, and Helplessness

Given that self-assertion is met by unkind cutting back, critique, or a lack of interest, needed autonomy becomes embued with loss of the vital other, "Therefore, the patient associates the fear of abandonment with his *own capacity for assertion*" (Masterson, 1980, p. 19) (italics added). Passivity, hopelessness, and helplessness illustrate that being oneself and supporting oneself is dangerous to a needed other. An analysand of Dr. Masterson, after asserting herself with her roommate, stated:

> When it is most important to support myself, it is most difficult. I feel like doing it, I do it, and then immediately I cut off. I am scared to death of that other person, who causes me to give up and wipes me out, who pulls the wool over my eyes. For example, even if I do assert myself, as I did with my roommate, by the time I report it here in the interview something (the defensive self) has taken away the feeling, so there is no feeling. The anger is gone, so it is just empty reporting. The power of the negative force is unreal. When I am abused and taken advantage of, I react passively and then turn and attack myself.
>
> (Masterson, 1985, p. 33)

Emptiness and Void

According to Masterson, the feeling of emptiness and void[4] "is best described as one of terrifying inner emptiness or numbness…it springs partially from introjection of the mother's negative attitudes, leaving the patient devoid, or empty, of positive supportive introjects" (Masterson, 1980, p. 19). An esteem-sensitive (narcissistic) analysand of Dr. Masterson stated the experience as follows:

> My real self-image is all bound up with my clone image of myself and my mother like two octopuses…I'm nobody, an eggshell to be broken. My mother punched a hole in the shell and sucked out the inside. There's nothing there. I feel no directions, I'm drifting like a spaceship…There's nothing inside, no essence [deflated self].
>
> (1985, p. 46)

Defenses Against the Abandonment Depression

The various disorders of self desperately rely on "defense" mechanisms[5] to ensure psychic survival and to avoid the overwhelming affects inherent in the abandonment depression. For the borderline or separation-sensitive analysand, it's the denial of the reality of separation and avoidance of individuation stimuli; for the esteem-sensitive or narcissistic disorder of self, it's the denial and avoidance of the rapprochement crisis, i.e., the reliance on a continuously activated defense of grandiosity and perfection as a defense against the deflated self. For the contact-sensitive analysand or the schizoid disorder of self, it's the fear that connection and contact may bring appropriation, that being with another evokes insatiable need, love turned hungry, and that exile is the only option in having some psychic life. Lastly, the symbiotic or emergent sensitive analysand in search of an organizing experience may abruptly experience impingement, petrification, and psychic implosion (à la R.D Laing), evoking dedifferentiation, perceptual disturbance, and autistic-like adaptations. "Defenses" come alive in the therapeutic encounter for Masterson in the so-called *disorders of self triads*.

Disorders of Self Triads

Within Masterson's meticulous psychoanalytic work, the psychological rhythms of the disorders of self, as they are informed and reflect developmental needs and conflicts, enabled Masterson to find an inherent "logic" in each of the disorders of self. The triads (see figures below) can be argued as the unseen gravitational fields organizing the analysand's intrapsychic and interpersonal lives as they navigate adult lives. An example may suffice. If you imagine four analysands with similar articulation but from within *four* different Mastersonian languages of self-algorithms:

> Analysand: I feel in two – a part of me wants to get better, to live fuller (Masterson's Real self), but every time I do… (self-activation)
>
> I feel I will be left alone, even abandoned by you (borderline dilemma/ separation-sensitive)
>
> I may be found inadequate and not intelligent enough – an intellectual imposter and imperfect (narcissistic dilemma/ esteem-sensitive)
>
> I will feel compelled to have to spend more time with my partner, which makes me feel smothered and as if they expect more of me, makes me feel beholden to her needs; I then wish to be single again, alone (schizoid dilemma/contact-sensitive)
>
> I become divided. "I am" in boasting for God, being good. Then getting rageful, not being seen for my sacrifice, all the memories of my faith grief- God and Satan against me. Damaging acts against my little person. They send me to the pit; hell is real and terrible. Drove me to suicide; they stoned and killed my soul, murdered my soul. I was gone for days after trying to kill myself (dedifferentiation after a psychotic delusion) (symbiotic dilemma, coming-into-being)

The example just provided could be written in the following triad- logic:

Symbiotic (awakening/emerging-sensitive) triad

Coming-into-being↔dedifferetiation↔autistic retreat

Schizoid (contact-sensitive) triad

Connection↔danger↔safe distance

Narcissistic (esteem-sensitive) triad

Imperfection↔painful vulnerability↔grandiosity

Borderline (separation-sensitive) triad

Competence/Individuation↔abandonment↔regression

The triads enable the analytic listener to enter the developmental needs and conflicts, feel, and "hear" the struggles anew – whether speaking from the emerging, hatching, practicing, or rapprochement *eras and areas* of the psyche. Knowing the triads supports the analyst to adapt his attitude, approach, and analytic action to meet the analysand's developmental self and object relations needs.

Masterson's Communicative Matching Technique with the Impaired Self

As the disorder of self analysands become, over time, increasingly able to tolerate the activation of the Real Self, it is of great importance to support the *Impaired Real Self.* Even with much progress within the working-through of the painful abandonment depression affects, Masterson found that focusing exclusively on the differentiation from the object solely failed to support the impaired self.[6] Synoptically stated, the analysand's newly found capacities and emergent self requires matching from a trusted other. During the initial conceptualizations of emotional refueling or "communicative matching," Masterson returned to the work of Mahler to understand this clinical dilemma:

> Two issues seem to be condensed in the refueling: (1) providing the child with the required feeling of closeness and acceptance, and (2) also providing emotional acknowledgement and support for the child's unfolding real self as seen in his or her self-assertive explorations. This is demonstrated dramatically in the rapprochement phase when the child repetitively piles all his new toys in his mother's lap for her acknowledgment.
>
> (Masterson, 1985, p. 57)

Activating and sustaining the self, in reality, remains a painful and arduous experience for the disorder of self analysand, frequented by inner doubts and lack of holding intrapsychic parental imagos. To counter such inner loneliness and struggle, the analysand may need the availability of the therapist to support the *Real Self* through the process of "communicative matching,"

> It is important to keep in mind that the objective of the communicative matching is to help the patient with the *quality of what he feels* – i.e., spontaneity, enthusiasm, excitement, vigor – as much as with what he does – i.e., self-assertive, supportive adaptive efforts.
>
> (Masterson, 1985, p. 61) (italics added)

This process, however, excludes all attempts to intimidate, force, direct, or seduce the client into activation of the *Real Self*. The main aim for the therapist is to serve as an intrapsychic buffer and guardian against the withdrawing (borderline), aggressively fused (narcissism), diabolically submerging (symbiotic), or sadistic-object and self-in-exile (schizoid) part-object relations units as the patient works through his abandonment depression affects. It is held that by serving as a psychological midwife, the *Real Self* may experience a sense of developmental competence, much needed to withstand the erosive qualities in general living. In Masterson's own words, as the abandonment depression has been attenuated and difficulties with self-activation emerge:

> I now stopped interpreting the abandonment depression and began to discuss with the patient—*to share or provide a form of communicative matching* with—the reality aspects of this new interest, providing a form of communicative matching by sharing whatever I might know about it and making a particular point of including, if possible, in my remarks some "lessons in life" about how effective adaptation works. The developmental arrest of the ego, with its ego defects and primitive mechanisms of defense, functions at the cost of reality perception. It is as if this part of the patient's personality had been left in the closet, locked away from learning contact with the environmental stimuli. Meanwhile, the rest of the patient's personality grew—i.e., his body, his intellect, his social behavior; though still dominated by the developmental arrest, these aspects had more adaptive capacity.
>
> (Masterson, 1985, p. 58)

The following section serves as "realities," when required, to be openly explored with the patient as they, although seemingly "common sense" to most, were never worked through with the disorder of self analysand. The areas to be addressed to support the impaired Real Self may be as follows:

Work

1. The more work fits your desire and natural aptitude, the more enhancing work will be to further psychological growth.
2. "Experimenting" with work, one's soul craft may be necessary to find what one desires.
3. True and lasting "success" concerning work requires initiative, self-assertion, repetitive effort, much "honing and refining," remaining buoyant after failures, continuous learning from mistakes, and recommitting oneself to one's soul-craft after success and failure (Masterson, 1985, p. 58).

Relationships

1. A good enough relationship takes both time and experimentation.
2. The degree of natural fit should include the reality of the other person's personality.
3. The closer the relationship develops, the more caution should be given concerning emotional involvement, balanced by the open communication of difficulty.
4. Although seemingly common sense, it is important to mourn the end of a close relationship before undertaking another (Masterson, 1988, pp. 58–59).

For Masterson, "The patients experienced these interventions as an *acknowledgment and refueling of their real self* and would then *pursue* the new interest with persistence, continuity and equally important, *a new sense of spontaneity, entitlement and vigor*" (1985, p. 59) (italics added).

The Therapeutic Frame and Process: Transference, Transference Acting Out, and the Therapeutic Alliance in Treating the Disorders of Self

For Masterson, transference is based on whole object relations and is the product of a relatively successful separation-individuation process. Whole object relations support the ability to reflect on one's own state of mind constructively, have a coherent theory of mind of another, and differentiate reality from one's feelings, thoughts, and actions. An analysand reflecting on their frustration at their analyst illustrates transference clearly:

> [Laughing] I wonder why, when you mentioned your observations, I suddenly experience you as critical- like my own father. This is difficult for me- I know the way you said it was not critical- it was a sudden flash feeling! It reminded me of my father.

Due to pre-Oedipal developmental lack and conflict, disorders of self analysands do not possess whole object relations and have not achieved object constancy. As such, the disorders of self analysands relate to others and the world mainly through projections,

> instead of seeing the therapist and the therapeutic situation realistically, they project one of their part object relations units onto the therapy, with its attendant part self- and object-representations and associated affects. They react then, often becoming shocked, disappointed, withdrawn, clingy, or even angry when the therapist does not act in accordance with their projections.
>
> (Masterson et al., 2004, p. 30)

The intrapsychic situation is based on a developmental arrest which limits the analysand's ability to see and experience others complexly. This arrest also casts a shadow over their ability to identify their wants and needs and act on them (to self-activate). For the pre-Oedipal analysand to survive and remain connected with the primary object implies having to comply, fuse, or give up their individuation.

According to Masterson, and based on the beforementioned arrest, the therapeutic alliance is possible once the analysand has internalized the analyst as a positive external other that supports the separation-individuation process. It is achieved mainly due to the working-through process wherein the patient can relate to the therapeutist and their own embattled, traumatized reality ego. Before such a state is possible, the analysand is subject to therapeutic acting out. Even within the working-through process, therapeutic acting out is expected to resurface, calling attention to the re-working of developmental dilemmas, although usually in tandem with communicative matching. Many volumes written by Masterson and clinicians such as Susan Kavaler-Adler (2003, 2017) attest to this process in detailed clinical studies and reflect the hard work of becoming one's self.

Analytic Neutrality and the Phases of Therapy

The aim of analytic neutrality, contrary to the perceived idea of the analyst being cold, aloof, and distant, is to create a therapeutic climate and setting of non-judgmental *attentiveness*, psychoanalytic support, and guarding against types of caretaking behaviors (i.e., being directive) which could stifle separation-individuation. The aim, in essence, is to serve as a *guardian to the Real Self.* For Masterson, this can be achieved, in a somewhat oversimplified way, within three therapeutic stages, although the stages will be influenced if the therapy is short or longer-term in nature. Longer-term psychotherapy would give the analysand and analyst significant opportunity with phases two and three, respectively.

For Masterson, **Stage 1** is typically characterized by *Testing* and *Transference Acting Out*. During this stage, the analysand enters therapy with their ego-syntonic ways of acting out their part-object units as a desperate attempt to ward off intrapsychic pain. Little continuity exists between sessions, and the analysand will test the analyst's ability to not collude with part units. The frame, as described by Robert Langs (1976, 1978 a&b, 1980) and others, is of extreme importance in this phase of therapy. The various techniques to be discussed in the upcoming chapters aim at turning ego-syntonic defenses ego-alien, so that the analysand can begin to have access to the multiple affects that motivate and mobilize ego defenses. The therapeutic alliance steadily grows out of this therapeutic phase.

During **Stage 2**, the *Working Through Phase*, there is less pressure on the analyst to interpret acting out. However, its reoccurrence is expected as the experience of the abandonment depression, and its associated memories necessitate further defense. Given the intensities of the work, sessions are usually added to contain the re-working and integration of pre-Oedipal trauma.

In **Stage 3**, *Termination* commences once "the patient's growth as a separate, unique individual has resumed" (Masterson et al., 2004, p. 34). Whole object relationships are possible, as are self-activation, creativity, intimacy, and the ability to tolerate depressive affects. As termination reactivated themes of separation for both parties, both analyst and analysand continue their journey in tolerating loss and cultivating gratitude in the analytic process and the transformative power of creative union.

Countertransference and Projective Identification – Communication by Impacts

Given the demands on the analyst vis-à-vis the projections of the various object relations units to be discussed in the chapters to come, countertransference experiences are to be expected. Masterson (1983) even goes as far as to write of its importance in the growth of the analyst himself, as many developmental difficulties faced in the disorders of self are perennial human difficulties, if not tragedies. Two excellent studies may aid clinicians in studying Masterson's[7] 1983 work on countertransference, as well as his 1989 and 1995 integrated clinical works[8] with various colleagues. The work by Betan, Heim, Conklin, and Westen (2005), *Countertransference phenomena and personality pathology in clinical practice: an empirical investigation*, as well as Berg & Lundh's (2022) *General patterns in psychotherapists' countertransference*, articulate many of the difficulties to be held in dealing with disorder of self analysands. The themes and factors include (a) feeling overwhelmed, if not disorganized, stimulating a need to avoid the analysand, (b) feeling inadequate, incompetent, and helpless, (c) feeling overinvolved and special, struggling to maintain boundaries, (d) struggling with sexualized, if nor eroticized, countertransference, (e) feeling disengaged, withdrawn, distracted, and bored, (f) feeling parental and protective stimulating unnecessary nurturance, and (g) feeling criticized, mistreated, unappreciated, dismissed, and/or devalued by the analysand. In the coming chapters, the reader may recognize some countertransference reactions just mentioned, if not projectively identified with, as deep communications from the split internal world of the disorder of self analysands.

Notes

1 As described by Mahler and McDevitt (1982), "I will assume the infant has two basic points of reference from which he builds up his self-schema: one, his own inner feelings or states forming the primitive core of the self on the one hand and, two, his sense of the care given by the libidinal object on the

other hand. Insofar as the infant's development of the sense of self takes place in the context of the dependency on the mother, the sense of self that results will bear the imprint of her caregiving" (p. 837).

2 For an in-depth discussion on Masterson's positioning of Winnicott in his work, see the section, *True and False Self* (Winnicott), in the volume, *The Narcissist and Borderline Disorders* (1981), pp. 106–108.

3 See Eigen's affect trilogy *Rage* (2002), *Ecstasy* (2001), and *Lust* (2006) for an in-depth psychoanalytic exploration.

4 Another example from the psychoanalyst Peter Lomas: "Now I know what I am. Everything I have ever done has been to please people. But I didn't ask to be born, did I? A plastic bag was put on me and I couldn't get out of it. Is that the womb or what is it? I've never escaped from my mother. I'm just her and there's nothing of me. I can only go on living if I forget all about this. Otherwise it's just a vacuum, emptiness, nothing. I've got to forget this if I can fit in again. My life's all been tricks. I never stop trying to make people like me" (1973, p. 104).

5 Orcutt's 2012 volume discusses in detail each disorder of self's use of various defense mechanisms such as denial, splitting, avoidance, and more.

6 The developmental importance of supporting self-activation and growth was also described by Frank Summers and can be read in his creative work *Self Creation. Psychoanalytic Therapy and the Art of the Possible*, published in 2005.

7 Although I mention these three volumes specifically, most of Masterson's volumes address countertransference realities.

8 Masterson, J. F. (1983). *Countertransference and Psychotherapeutic Technique*. New York: Brunner/Mazel.

Masterson, J. F., & Klein, R. (1989). *Psychotherapy of the Disorders of the Self. The Masterson Approach.* New York: Brunner/Mazel.

Masterson, J. F., & Klein, R. (1995). *Disorders of the Self. New Therapeutic Horizons. The Masterson Approach.* New York: Brunner/Mazel.

Part 2

Union in Development

Symbiosis and the Foundations of Primal Organizing Connection

Chapter 4

On Psychological Beginnings

Candace Orcutt's Mastersonian Approach to the Symbiotic Experience

Introduction

Masterson's developmental self and object relations approach and meticulous tracking of connection-separation-individuation cycles enabled Dr. Candace Orcutt, a psychoanalyst, traumatologist, and central collaborator of Masterson, to expand his thinking to the earliest, pre-Mahlerian separation-individuation, states of mind[1] (Orcutt and Daws, in press). That is, not only is the Masterson Approach applicable to the domain of disorders of the self, but Masterson's thinking[2] can be successfully applied to the earliest states of psychic organization and experience. Brevity necessitates a very narrow approach in this chapter. However, Masterson's earliest work, as well as Orcutt's 1989 chapter, will include many scholars such as Sigmund Freud, Heiman Spotnitz, and many others.

Orcutt and Masterson on the Pre-Separation-Individuation Dilemma

In the developmental model proposed by Mahler (borrowing from Freud and later elaborated), the *metaphor* of an egg[3] did help differentiate between two subphases of primary narcissism. In the first three months, *normal autism* was argued to find the infant unaware of the mothering other. In contrast, in the symbiotic stage proper (three months onwards), the "infant begins dimly to perceive need satisfaction as coming from a need-satisfying part object" (Mahler, 1967, pp. 79–80).

DOI: 10.4324/9781003358572-6

The developmental shift is conceptually brought about progressively by a maturational crisis wherein the infant's stimulus barrier experiences radical changes, that is, "the quasi-solid stimulus barrier...*this autistic shell*[4], which kept external stimuli out—begins to crack," and in its place "a positively cathected stimulus shield begins to form and to envelop the symbiotic orbit of the *mother-child dual unity*" (Mahler, 1967, pp. 83–84) (italics added). Interpersonally then, the very specific smiling response as found in the symbiotic phase can be argued as an acknowledgment of mother-infant relatedness; *mother as a symbiotic partner*, a "symbiotic organizer"[5] (Mahler, 1966, p. 60; 1967, p. 81), or a "protective living shield" (quoting Rene Spitz) against stimuli and functions as the infant's "(external) auxiliary executive ego" (Mahler, 1966, p. 60), "the beacon of orientation in the world of reality," a "'symbiotic membrane' of the mother-child dual unity" (Mahler, 1966, p. 62) mediating the vulnerable infant's growing capacity to perceive and relate to both the internal and the outer "worlds." It is essential to keep in mind that for Mahlerian psychoanalysis: "Only if symbiosis has been adequate, is [the infant] ready to enter the phase of gradual separation and individuation [and achieve] a stable image of the self" (Mahler & Gosliner, 1955, p. 111). The function of the mothering other as a developmental protector is essential, without which the rudimentary ego cannot approach the demands of differentiation and separation. The essential *oneness* and *all is me (union)*, to the vague sense of a need-satisfying and calming object is dependent on the ever-accumulating memory islands (based on pleasurable good and painful bad stimuli) of good and bad sensations, the precursors of the earliest feelings states (however scattered). Both Orcutt and Mahler mention that the primordial "feeling" states are not necessarily transported to "self," "nonself," and "object" states in the earliest symbiotic epoch, but in time, "The confluence and primitive integration of the scattered 'good' and 'bad' memory islands into two large, good and bad part images of the self, as well as split good and bad part images of the mother" (Mahler & Gosliner, 1955, p. 114) and will only be evident by the second year of life. It is difficult to truly "know," from an object relations point of view, the actual impact, given the lack of a harmonious symbiotic organizer, or the disorganization experienced (fueled by an impingement-lack dialectic) being exposed to a parasitic organizer on the self-other formation of the infant. In the work of many, the world of perdition and the diabolical may come to mind,[6] reflecting the need for autistic retreats, encapsulation, and psychotic withdrawal.

Orcutt on the Pathological Model

Orcutt, similar to Mahler, mentions that when considering such symbiotic developmental difficulty, a complex interplay exists between constitutional ego defects in the infant and the possibility of ego defects in the mother.[7,8] Ego defects in the mothering other may be evident in over-anxiousness and overprotectiveness, to the most disturbing lack of affect transmission and psycho-physical neglect (a woodenness).[9] Pioneering the earliest studies on childhood psychosis, Mahler differentiates between the autistic and the symbiotic-psychotic child and writes that whereas in the autistic-psychotic child, there seems to be a lack of interest in the human world, the symbiotic-psychotic child, "begins to show some picture of regression to a point of ego fixation" wherein one can assume some object relatedness did take part (Orcutt, in Masterson et al., 1989, p. 114). For Mahler, the symbiotic-psychotic child may thus make use of autistic defenses *to protect* a minimal self (incipient ego) from engulfment/impingement. That is, the symbiotic-psychotic child protects him/herself "from the challenge of separate functioning at the onset or during the separation-individuation phase into a symbiotic-parasitic, panic-ridden state" (Mahler & Furer, 1960, p. 223). Orcutt, who also worked with adolescent and adult schizophrenic experiences, found a similar withdrawal (Orcutt's "psyche's falling back," see Orcutt in Masterson et al., 1989, p. 114) from the world under the pressure of similar maturational-emancipation challenges.

For Orcutt and Masterson, the psychotic defense may be a reactive restitution wherein a beleaguered ego may attempt to move to earlier experiences and resources wherein a oneness with the object may be possible (with a promise of rebirth from the omnipotently fused dual unity?). Despite such a reality, psychotic object relationships are "restitutional attempts of a rudimentary or fragmented ego which serve the purpose of survival...as no human being can live in an objectless state" (Mahler & Furer, 1960, p. 192), and

> We often find...a debilitating emotional unavailability on the part of the mother because she has a depression. We also find, at the opposite pole, an interference with the infant's gratification-frustration experiences, a stifling of his budding ego, by a smothering disregard of his need to experience gratification and frustration at his own pace.
> (Mahler, 1965, p. 161)

Thus, similar to the momentous work of Sullivan (1953) and others, the protective movement, in effect, reflects developmental and individuation conflicts based on a self-system that learned that the environment could not (or will not) scaffold the *symbiotic-emergent self*,

> The pathogenic effect of the attitude of the symbiotically over-anxious mother is particularly increased if that mother's hitherto doting attitude *changes abruptly at the advent of the separation-individuation phase*...A complementary pathogenic factor is the well-known, parasitic, infantilizing mother who needs to continue her overprotection beyond the stage where it is beneficial.
>
> (Mahler & Gosliner, 1955, p. 116) (italics added)

Orcutt's Clinical Picture

Orcutt's work beautifully illustrates how experiencing a symbiotic-psychotic episode, mainly in her work with schizophrenic analysands, clinically presents as

> someone desperately trying to establish a *symbiotic bond* to *undo ego disintegration* in the face of severe separation stress. The therapist's function is to *ally with* the schizophrenic patient at the symbiotic level of functioning and to strengthen this position so that higher levels of adaptation can be *reclaimed or newly established.*
>
> (Orcutt, in Masterson, 1989, p. 116) (italics added)

Given such developmental "dis"-stress and strain, how could a developmentally needed adaptation be reclaimed or newly established? For Orcutt, the first area of focus would be to *actively facilitate a symbiotic transference*. For those trained in Masterson, this would imply sensitively meeting the transference acting out, holding the projection upon the analyst of the patient's inner world. As will be evident in later chapters, the transference acting out in the symbiotic transference is largely a psychotic transference

> in which the distinction between the patient's projections and the reality of the therapist (along with any other self and object differentiations) effectively disappears. In other words, there is only a trace of a working alliance, which must *be painstakingly developed*

> from a positive symbiotic transference into which the negative is gradually integrated.
>
> (Orcutt, in Masterson et al., 1989, p. 116)

Furthermore, the projection of the internal world is a *dedifferentiated* one, reflecting a general lack of separation between self and other, and a clear split between good and bad. Being symbiotically fixated on the family of origin[10] (through enmeshment as a defense) allowed rudimentary, although fragile, adaptations. Inevitable separation stresses and other external pressures for emancipation find a catastrophic lack of auxiliary environmental support and the unfortunate symbiotic-psychotic individual unable to sustain the false defensive self. The symbiotic structure may become increasingly evident. Being unable to find or rely on adequate, differentiated, and vitalizing self and object representations in the internal world able to fuel separation and emancipation, "The remaining fragment of the patient's self makes a pathological alliance with the therapist in a symbiotic transference that defends against the sense of *dissolution*" (Orcutt, in Masterson et al., 1989, p. 117). Such annihilation anxiety must be an unimaginable state of being.

Despite the importance of the symbiotic bond as a protection against further dissolution, the bond also contains twin fears, mimicking the ontogenic push to separation-individuation. Mahler (referring to the treatment of children) observed that the very need for the "restoration of the omnipotent oneness with the symbiotic mother" also serves as the basis for "a panicky fear of fusion and of dissolution of the self" (1965, p. 162). An electrified developmental tightrope needed to be navigated analytically so that the analysand can, in time, reliably test and adapt to reality and the symbiotic other at their own pace; "it is important to *let the [patient] test reality* very *gradually at his own pace*" (Mahler, 1952, p. 152) with the aim of a *corrective symbiotic experience*. This corrective symbiotic experience may protect against further annihilation anxiety and dissolution of the nascent self. It is hoped that the analysand can build a more stable intrapsychic structure by gradually "regathering" islands of good and bad feelings in the therapeutic holding environment. As the islands of good accumulate, it will be followed by a fear that the bad may overtake the good, and "Once this good and bad split inner world is established, the patient begins to renegotiate the pathological equivalent of the differentiation subphase of separation-individuation" (Orcutt, in Masterson et al., 1989, p. 118). Orcutt supports the therapist in mentioning that the work needed on this level is immensely challenging. The therapist must be willing to "hear with the left ear"[11] "and perceive with the right, intuitive hemisphere. At the same time, of course, it is imperative that the therapist's ego remain firmly established in reality" (Orcutt, in Masterson et al., 1989, p. 118). In early treatment, the analyst provides a setting wherein the primary function may be summarized as follows:

- Restitution of the stimulus barrier, enabling a homeostatically supported ambiance[12] able to support the building of psychic structure. As a symbiotic partner, the analyst-mother remains an external background organizer in the analysands' most unique awake feeding (presence and words), structuring (pain-satiation), and sleep (conscious-unconscious) rhythms on the way to eventual hatching, practicing, and transitional relatedness. The rhythm, evident in *joining presencing*[13] to be discussed, brings the syncretistic and concrete ego with its potential into the "safe" maternal envelope, enabling worlding and the reinstitution of ego expansion-contraction rhythms, our common projective and introjective identification mechanisms.
- Once relative safety seems possible, even through extended periods of silence from the analyst, the analyst may initiate and encourage whatever forms of connection and contact the analysand can tolerate and allow through the technique of joining as described by Spotnitz (1985) and his followers.
- Joining may, with time, be followed by *mirroring*, supporting gentle *differentiation*[14] between self and other. However, mirroring is expected to bring about earlier lack and terror, which is to be held and processed.

With *joining*, the central attitude and intervention focus on affective congruence (safety for union). As developed by Spotnitz, in time, mirroring techniques[15] can be relied upon to support needed differentiation (distinction). Given the sensitivity of hatching, "verbal" feedings, as Spotnitz would write, should be kept to a minimum. Despite the clinician's most sensitive tending to psychic movement, all interventions disrupt the oceanic merger and become part of hatching pain.

To summarize, in the early stages of analysis, the patient may derive a sense of safety from the therapist's joining. Such protection may sufficiently halt the regressive descent of the illness. As treatment continues, the analysand may begin to make a reconstitutive ascent, during which an implicit sense of alliance (union) is added to the symbiotic transference and hints at the growth of an underlying interpersonal process. Differences of opinion are allowed (if not welcomed), and a sense of developing intrapsychic structure emerges. Now the therapist must be alert to this shift to meet it constructively with a change of interventions: from joining to mirroring to confrontation and other ego-supportive, self-acknowledging approaches, and here-and-now interpretations. This sequence will not be steady but, rather, will be interrupted by sporadic regressions, when joining and mirroring will again be necessary. For Orcutt,

> Interventions are made at points of resistance, specifically, the patient's resistance to being in the session, or talking in the session, or to allowing the fostering of the symbiotic transference. Successful interventions, by helping the patient to resolve anxieties that interfere with verbalizing, limit the acting out of these resistances.
>
> (Masterson et al., 1989, p. 121)

The Intrapsychic Structure

Whereas the disorders of self imply a certain degree of endopsychic differentiation (of self and object representations that oscillate), the analysands described here either experience a defensive dedifferentiation of self and object representations or reflect a deficit in representational development able to tolerate oscillating part units on the way to whole and constant object relatedness. Although never fully formalized into a workable pictogram[16,17] (as seen with the other disorders of self in chapters to follow), I do propose the following based on the work of Dr. Orcutt.

As mentioned, the self and object representations start as rudimentary pleasure-unpleasure states. One could visually represent it as follows S+ (pleasurable self-states), S− (non-pleasurable self-states), O+ (pleasurable other), O− (unpleasant others) that will, in time, build to pleasurable self-other and displeasurable self-other. The two experiences will also be influenced by infantile omnipotence and need, serving as the basis for the Divine S+–O+ unit and the Diabolical S− – O− unit.[18] Environmental and internal stress can also lead to variations and adaptations in the representational units, that is, diabolical self and

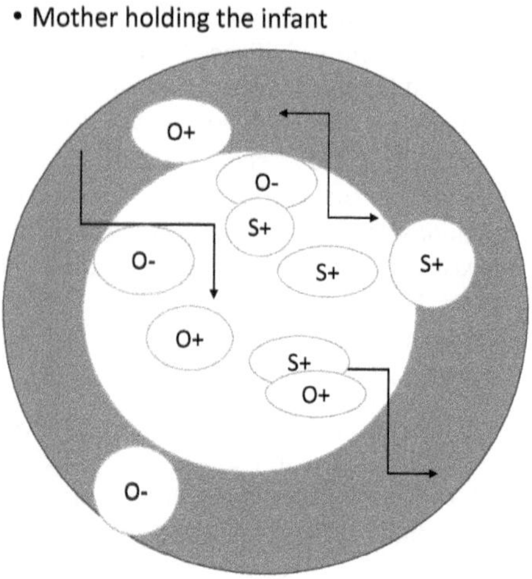

• Mother holding the infant

Figure 4.1 Fused Object Relations Unit of the Symbiotic (Psychotic) Disorder of Self.

divine other ("I am Satan, should be punished," as in psychotic depressions), to divine self and diabolical others ("I am Jesus and must be sacrificed"). Given the large amount of divine self-experience in hospitalized schizophrenics, one can remain hopeful of a "core" goodness. In terms of Masterson's thinking, one could also write; diabolical SR> (not fused but "swallowed") by the diabolical OR, diabolical SR< (not fused, swallowing) the diabolical OR, and many more permutations so evident in early mythologies. It is also of interest to note that the earliest unconscious representation of the psychotic self-other frequently includes mythological figures, some from gods, that are half human and half animal, representing either the fusion with the instincts or the minimal ego differentiation from the Id, and include the centaurs, the gorgons, mermaids, the minotaur, even the modern Freudian Sphinx! Such pleasure-unpleasure and diabolical-divine experiences are evident in Freud's work on Judge Schreber and many of Jung's conceptualizations. Succinctly stated, this is the world of the *Divine Child* and *pre-dates* Ferenczi's concept of the *Wise Child*, which could be ascribed to the schizoid dilemma to be discussed in the next chapter.[19] Given the fragile nature of the original units and the immaturity of the perceptual system, dedifferentiation[20] remains an ever-present option and threat. Not only can autistic-like retreats threaten further differentiation, but the psyche may be exposed to a schizophrenic world and, at worst, to the domain of catatonia.

Case Illustration – Ruth and Dr. Orcutt

Ruth[21] (a pseudonym) was referred to the Masterson Group at age 20. Synoptically, Ruth experienced her first psychotic experience at 16 and again at 18 as she attempted to study away from home (separation stress). During her last hospitalization, Ruth exhibited catatonic motor behavior and was found curled inside a clothing dryer (in search of a symbiotic experience, container, womb?). According to Orcutt's conceptualization, based on Ruth's angry acting out, ominous threats, combined with various retreat behaviors and mute protests,

> Her dilemma made no sense in terms of the whole self and other object relations but was clear in emotional terms: she was trapped between persecutory and idealized states[22] (extreme, primitive states of good and bad), which fluctuated in their attachment to part self and object representations. The element of her that was "*missing" was the capacity of the self to begin to organize these states into separate camps, with attachment to distinct self and other part representations.*
>
> (Orcutt, in Masterson et al., 1989, pp. 123–124)

In an attempt to organize a frightful inner world, Ruth obsessively reasoned out her situation. Orcutt's attempts at assistance (interpretation as a medium) evoked barely contained aggressive impulses, i.e., throwing at Dr. Orcutt with her purse. Such moments were met with *mirroring*; "Mirroring, I said I thought I had disrupted the flow of the session, and she relaxed and continued her verbal puzzling over her dilemma" (Orcutt, in Masterson et al., 1989, p. 124). Mirroring was aided by *joining*[23] Ruth's struggle, at times in silent validation, scaffolding Ruth's ego-enhancing "striving for meaning" (Orcutt, in Masterson et al., 1989, p. 124) whereby "Her obsessive persistence with definitions of right and wrong was essentially a side-product of her need to organize her perception of good and bad in the 'world.'" (Orcutt, in Masterson et al., 1989, p. 124) As mentioned, accepting and joining the struggle allows the clinician a unique development opportunity in scaffolding the symbiotic ego-self function of boundary formation and self-other differentiation. It is expected to lower anxiety, strengthen a maturational need for self-trust, and meet further developmental storms to come. The following serves as an imaginal therapeutic interaction from the written material in the 1989 Masterson edition, dialogically indicating a successful symbiotic transference.

Symbiotic Transference

Ruth: [Holding Dr. Orcutt's pillow] "Your pillow matches my dress. May I take it home with me?" [symbiotic statement and wish]
Orcutt: "Should I come home with you and bring my pillow?"
Ruth: [Nonverbal] Smiling, able to leave without the pillow. Words had bridged the separation.

Use of Therapeutic Self to Differentiate Anger

Ruth: [Silent]
Orcutt: [Reflecting that she did not help Ruth articulate] "Perhaps the only helpful thing I have done is to let you hold my pillow."
Ruth: [Laughing, reflecting the validating "consensus laugh," as Masterson notes.] "I'm trying to break away from part of myself—acting against part of myself that's restrictive." [talking more differentiated on anger and self].

Furthermore, central to working with the symbiotic sphere, is relaxation in the service of growth:

> As she relaxed, she began to tolerate more give and take and became interested in discussing more characterological issues, her perfectionism in particular. She discussed concepts of 'moderation' and 'extreme' and was interested in continuing *our* "scientific" talks. She began to show interest in me as a person, asking about my professional orientation (I told her). She began to allow me to be more *responsive*.
>
> (Orcutt, in Masterson et al., 1989, p. 125)

In months to come, various changes indicated greater awareness of inner and outer reality and of the therapeutic relationship. Ruth sent a note apologizing for abusing Dr. Ocutt "as a person *and* a therapist" (p. 125), acknowledging the importance that Dr. Orcutt understood the latter as a reaction to feeling "trapped." The growing awareness of the impact, sensing the inner world of the analyst, and her own inner-outer reality conflicts and stresses brought new challenges, such as her own observation that she needed to be more social and return to school. In this period, Ruth accepted *clarifying statements* from Dr. Orcutt, such as Ruth couldn't "understand the inner world without attending to the outer world, too...The fact that I could make a clarifying statement of that sort indicated how much she had allowed us to differentiate and to exchange opinions" (Orcutt, in Masterson et al., 1989, p. 125). After a mere 18 months, Ruth returned to her previous level of functioning "I almost feel good—closer to who I am." Success, the therapeutic achievement "had not come primarily from insight into a puzzle (the outward form it took) but, rather, from a therapeutically supported step forward, based on the patient's need for a *validating emotional unity* with the therapist" (Orcutt, in Masterson et al., 1989, p. 126).

Countertransference and the Difficulties in Holding the Symbiotic Analysand

As succinctly written by Spotnitz, moving from a rudimentary to a cooperative relationship entails a particular sensitivity and approach; "Usually he labours under the unconscious conviction of having been an 'unwanted child,'[24] and enters the office steeled against the expectation of insistent probing and wounding inspection" (1985, p. 113). Technically, Harry Stack Sullivan writes,

> Per contra, if you have to deal with schizophrenia, then this formulation of mine implies the importance of carefully putting almost a scaffolding under the patient's self-system in its relation to you – that is, establishing a 'me-you' pattern, if you please, between yourself and the patient which is of an utterly previously *unexperienced solidity and dependability*.[25] Only then can you get to the point where you can deal with disturbing material without causing this sudden disturbance of the self-function of suppressing more primitive types of mental process, with, as a result, the abolition of communication and God knows what results in the patient, in the sense of what finally comes out as a result of your efforts.
>
> (1953, p. 363)

Such unexperienced solidity and dependability in the face of being unwanted do pose many countertransferential challenges – to such an extent that even Freud himself, in his many letters to Wilhelm Flies, referred to working with narcissistic transference and psychotic patients as the science of "dreckology" (in Spotnitz, 1985, p. 225), also finding Freud protecting himself by taking substances, keeping alive his sympathetic nervous system and suppressing any hostility and hate toward some of his psychotic patients. For Searles,

> One of the surest criteria I have discovered, by which I know that a patient is schizophrenic, is my finding that I tend to experience myself as being nonhuman in relation to him - to feel for example, that I *emerge*, in relation to him, as being so inhumanly callous or sadistic, or so *filled with weird fantasies within myself, as to place me well outside the realm of human beings.*
>
> (1979, p. 285) (italics added)

Typical countertransference[26,27] realities include, but are not limited to, (a) hastening the analysand toward rational and secondary process understanding (from the Parataxic Level to the Syntaxic Level à la Sullivan), (b) disconnecting and closing off emotional contact out of fear[28] and/or repulsion, (c) messianic fervor in curing the patient with words and understanding, (d) experiencing various primordial bodily sensations – at times autistic, at times charged with erotic and hateful (diabolical) intensity as to be felt disorganizing, (e) body and mental ego experiences of unintegrated states of mind (falling, dissolving, spilling), and more. The work of the theorists mentioned, as well as keeping in mind the Mastersonian *psychotic triad*, that is, emergence from the protective, if not defense symbiosis, may give rise to the awareness of contact with the diabolical other necessitating autistic-like adaptations and defenses (retreats, encapsulation, somatic inversion, severe mind-body splits, automaton behavior) may require the analyst to remain psychologically open to the experience of both psychotic and neurotic anxieties. Such openness and receptivity remain a considerable demand, yet transformative to all involved (Eshel, 2019).

Notes

1 Hamilton, F.J., & Masterson, Jr., J.F. (1958). Management of psychoses in general practice. *Medical Clinics of North America*, 42(3), 823–837.

2 "Unlike the autistic or infantile psychotic child, the child with a borderline syndrome has separated from the symbiotic stage and has become fixated in one of the subphases of the separation-individuation stage—possibly the rapprochement stage (15–22 months)" (Masterson, 1980, p. 20).
3 "A neat example of a psychical system closed off from the stimuli of the external world, and able to satisfy even its nutritional requirements autistically…is afforded by a bird's egg with its food supply enclosed in its shell; for it, the care provided by its mother is limited to the provision of warmth" (Mahler, 1967, p. 78).
4 Again, as evident in the work of Donald Stern and other researchers, the term "autistic" may be very misleading given their own research on infant development. However, when reviewing the metaphor, together with the outstanding volume of Albert Ciccone and Marc Lhopital entitled *Birth to Psychic Life* (2022), greater psychoanalytic care can be given to the work of Frances Tustin and Ester Bick on the auto-sensuous state, autistic state, the momentary object, and the autistic object as it relates to the work of Donald Meltzer, the French School, and American empirical traditions as they relate to the work of Mahler.
5 The volume entitled *The Search for Oneness,* written by L.H. Silverman, F.M. Lachmann, and R.H Milich, published in 1982, thickens much of Mahler's on symbiosis from within clinical psychoanalysis.
6 See the Jungian works of Henry Elkin (1958, 1972) and Michael Fordham (1994, 2019) as well as Margaret Cohen's work *Sent before My Time. A Child Psychotherapist's View of Life on a Neonatal Intensive Care Unit* (2003).
7 Dr. Galatzer-Levy (1988) argued that cycloid illnesses (manic depressive psychosis) can be understood as a disorder of the self. As a Kohutian psychoanalyst, Galatzer-Levy described various defects in the self of the cycloid patient, namely (a) the cycloid individual's defensive warding off of a *depletion depression*; (b) the use of language as mainly reflecting a disconnection between affect and experience; and (c) a unifying hypothesis integrating endowment and environmental/parental failure. Furthermore, the cycloid patient struggles with severe separation trauma, and in a desperate attempt to ensure others for intrapsychic equilibrium (referred to as "selfobjects"), inherent needs and wishes may be restricted, constricted, denied, and/or limited. This (seemingly) ensures constancy but at the expense of true self-expression and psychological vitality. This possibly reflects the aforementioned depletion depression:

> Manic-depressives seem to have much in common with patients with self-disorders. Self-object failures, both within and outside the analysis, threaten catastrophic experiences of loss of vitality, fragmentation, or both. At the same time they are unable to find adequate selfobjects. They may form relatively stable and sustaining selfobject relations by drastically constricting their needs. I suspect that the reluctance of these patients to enter psychotherapy and the (often conscious) care with which they select people to become involved with, reflects an acute awareness of the catastrophe that can ensue with selfobject failure. Mania and hypomanic states in these patients

appear as a defence against the dangers of the loss of the selfobject. These states are continuous with simple denial of the selfobject's importance; these difficulties come into particular prominence with separations. As I got to know the patients better, it seemed that a *depleted depression was more or less a chronic state of being for them.* Periods of supposedly good functioning were periods when denial worked adequately to manage depression. The anticipation of further and overwhelming depletion precipitated manic episodes, and depression was often more clearly manifest as the mania cleared. But generally these patients were constantly struggling with depression and attempting to keep it from becoming overwhelming (Galatzer-Levy, 1988, pp. 98–99; italics added).

8 The work of Jose Bleger, *Symbiosis and Ambiguity – A Psychoanalytic Study* (2013), remains a clinical and theoretical treasure. Bleger's thinking finds a unique conceptualization that argues for the reality that prior to Klein's paranoid-schizoid position, autism, and symbiosis co-exist as narcissistic relations in a syncretic "agglutinated" nucleus.
9 Please refer to Chapter 2 to review "qualities of mothering" and the role of both the maternal and paternal functions in structural development. Elkin's papers (1958, 1972) are also very helpful in this regard.
10 The work of psychiatrists and psychoanalysts Murray Bowen and R.D. Laing is of immense importance here.
11 Very similar to Bollas's approach in his two works, *Catch Them Before They Fall* (2012) and *When the Sun Bursts* (2015).
12 The use of silence, ambiance, tone of voice, calm (not detached), and minimal intrusive activity is important in the many stages in therapy. Monitoring of impact whilst remaining vitally present is difficult, and PI and CT should be monitored.
13 Also see the work of Hedges on the organizing experience (1994b), Searles on pre-ambivalent symbiosis (1965), Eigen's *Psychotic Core* (1986), Spotnitz's work on the narcissistic transference (1969) as well as the brilliant Jungian work of John Weir Perry in his two works, *The Self in Psychotic Process. Its Symbolization in Schizophrenia (1953)* and *The Far Side of Madness (1974).*
14 Eigen's 1986 chapter (8, pp. 313–363), *The Psychotic Self,* is of immense help clinically, articulating union and differentiation dilemmas as found in the psychotic self. Also see *Interventions and the Distinction-Union Structure* for thoughts on differentiation within the psychotic self, pp. 306–312.
15 Eigen's section entitled "Interventions and the Distinction-Union Structure" (1986, pp. 306–312) artfully describes the ability to work with differentiation and the dedifferentiation pull/fusional complex. Also see Chapter 8, the Psychotic Self (1986, pp. 313–363).
16 In the *Meaning of Anxiety in Psychiatry and in Life*, the great Harry Stack Sullivan (in *Psychiatry,* 1948, 11, pp. 1–13) does provide marvelous visual representations to depict "areas" of personality development and the

varieties of anxiety that can be integrated by the self-system. The interpersonal adds a unique combination of how such anxieties can transpire between two individuals. A truly classic work in psychoanalysis.

17 For excellent *developmental diagrams* from the theories of Kernberg and many others (pp. 204–205, 235, 241, 313, 369, 422–424), the reader is referred to an under appreciated text by Patricia M. Chatham (1985) *Treatment of the Borderline Personality* wherein many main theorists are discussed.

18 Also see the following volumes:

Sechehaye, M. (1951a). *Symbolic realization.* New York: International Universities Press.
Sechehaye, M. (1951b). *Autobiography of a Schizophrenic Girl.* New York: Grune & Stratton.

19 Also see the work of Christopher Fortune entitled *The Analytic Nursery: Ferenczi's 'Wise Baby' Meets Jung's 'Divine Child,'* published in 2003, for a detailed discussion

20 Also see Mahler, M.S., (1960). Perceptual dedifferentiation and psychotic object relations, Chapter 10, pp. 183–192, in *The Selected Papers of Margaret S. Mahler, M.D., Vol. 1.* New York: Jason Aronson, 1979.

21 The case of Ruth can be read in Masterson et al., 1989, pp. 122–126.

22 Although outside the scope of the current volume, the reader is referred to Orcutt's 2021 work, Diagram 6.1, p. 166. I believe that the diagram serves as a conceptual and theoretical bridge between the abovementioned figure and the schizoid split units diagram of Masterson.

23 Joining as described by Dr. Orcutt: "Joining is an intervention directed primarily to feeling, not reason, and context rather than content. (The metaphor, used by Spotnitz among others, is that of feeding the hungry infant; explaining what hunger is about simply does not meet the situation)" (in Masterson et al., 1989, p. 124).

24 Also see Ferenczi, S. (1929). The Unwelcome Child and his Death-Instinct. *International Journal of Psychoanalysis,* 10, 125–129.

25 In a section entitled *Postcript*, Margaret Little writes that "Trust in the analyst has had to be built up through experience of his reliability and general predictability. A good deal of repetition is often needed in the working through...The original damage cannot be undone, but providing other experiences to put *alongside* the earlier ones enables the patient to bring his more mature, nondelusional self into action" (1990, p. 106).

26 I exclude here the use and experience of positive countertransference as seen in the work of Brooke Laufer (2010), Beyond countertransference: Therapists' experiences in clinical relationships with patients diagnosed with schizophrenia *(Psychosis),* in *Psychological, Social and Integrative Approaches*, 2(2), 163–172.

27 The work of Margaret Little (1990), *Psychotic anxieties and containment. A personal record of an analysis with Winnicott,* discusses the impact of countertransference on the analysand in need of an organizing experience in much detail.

28 The affect fear I refer to here can be found in different levels of development and representation given the developmental model. Please see the work of Bernd Nissen, *'Emotional' Storms in Autistoid Dynamics*, chapter 6, pp. 113–128, in *Engaging Primitive Anxieties of the Emerging Self.* The legacy of Francis Tustin, edited by Howard B Levine and D.G. Power, as well as Steiner's *Psychic Retreats* and Spotnitz's narcissistic transference work.

Part 3

From Union to Distinction

Hatching and the Schizoid Dilemma

Chapter 5

Is There Anybody Out There?

Ontological Insecurity and the Search for a Safe Connection

Given the developmental theory of Dr. Masterson, Dr. Ralph Klein, the then medical director of the Masterson Institute, pioneered the developmental self and object relations approach to the schizoid dilemma. For Klein, the analysands under consideration did not seem to express similar developmental difficulties as evident in borderline or narcissistic dilemmas. Instead, they responded highly reactively, even fearfully, in connecting to others. In reviewing the seminal work of Drs. Ronald Fairbairn and Harry Guntrip, Klein found that the focus of schizoid analysands was not so much on the trauma of separating from the needed other, or the need for fusion and the reliance on idealized defenses, but rather, on a deep fear of connectedness, as being connected was experienced as being colonized. With this understanding and clinical orientation, Klein set out to map the intrapsychic dilemma of the schizoid within the Masterson tradition.

The Other as Appropriator Hatching Trauma and the Search for Safety

W.R.D. Fairbairn (1952), an immensely creative and independent Scottish psychoanalyst, single-handedly repositioned Freudian psychoanalysis by focusing on the infant's human need for the other, rather than the accepted conceptualizations based on libido being primarily "pleasure-seeking." As so beautifully written by Fairbairn's senior analysand Harry Guntrip, "The one thing that the child cannot do for himself is to give himself a basic sense of security, since that is a function of object relationship" (1969, p. 193). Given such a need,

DOI: 10.4324/9781003358572-8

the lack of human connection in environments characterized by possessiveness, indifference, and the smothering of a vibrant self, creates an inner life devoid of ontological security. To be loved and to reciprocate love with love and tenderness is an essential human interaction. Fairbairn writes as follows:

> The greatest need of a child is to *obtain conclusive assurance* (a) that he is *genuinely loved* as a person by his parents, and (b) that his parents genuinely *accept* his love…In the absence of such assurance, his relationships to his objects is fraught with *too much anxiety over separation* to enable him to renounce the attitude of infantile dependence: for such a renunciation would be equivalent in his eyes to forfeiting all hope of ever obtaining the satisfaction of his unsatisfied emotional needs. *Frustration of his desire to be loved as a person, and frustration of his desire to have his love accepted, is the greatest trauma that a child can experience.*
>
> Fairbairn, 1952, pp. 39–40) (italics added)

Similar to the work of analysts such as Ian Suttie (1935), Harry Stack Sullivan (1953), Masud Khan (1989, 1996), and contemporaries such as Michael Eigen (1986, 1999) and Ofra Eshel (2019), the creation of safety, security, and the protection of the nascent self remains *the* central task of the good enough environment. To return to Mahler, and thickened by the work of Ralph Klein (1995, in Masterson and Klein, 1995) and Candace Orcutt (2021), it can be conceptualized that the schizoid developmental dilemma can be found in the *hatching phase* of development wherein the mother's reciprocal mirroring creates an interpersonal situation where her needs and psychological preferences *supplant* that of the infant's. More specifically, it would seem that the sense of a *viable hatching self* is curtailed, stifled, or severely inhibited in order to be "congruent with the mother's degree of acceptance" (Orcutt, 2021, p. 8). Whereas spontaneous exploration is expected, the schizoid deals with maternal impingement, and the schizoid's adaptation moves from authenticity, being-in and with the world, to psychic "reactivity," detached observation, and even compliance. An analysand I will call Sarah reported:

> I observed my mother – especially her anger…I mainly observe and pick things up, but I have gotten in trouble saying what I feel…It's dangerous to say what you think and feel. My mother was always

> right, and I was always wrong. Do as she commands. It felt safer to withdraw and rather observe...My ostrich behavior...And I work so that I don't have to think [Guntrip's doing vs. being]...I fill myself then there is no danger to *feel me*, 'me' gets me into trouble...complying and going along is safer...*I feel like I am sitting IN myself.*

Orcutt adds that the mothering other's anxious, controlling, and impinging behavior curtails most environmental exploration, and submission feeds a rather reactive personality style.[1] Thus, moving from a position and experience of ontological insecurity, subject to a lack of marked affect mirroring, the true self remains hypersensitive to being marginalized and, at worst, appropriated. Self-preservation may also imply using various "techniques" to keep the other at bay while having some contact with the world, as the loss of connection would mean an experience of cosmic aloneness, unbearable for humans. As I have previously written (Daws, 2013), these techniques can be viewed on a continuum, the most severe being similar to the contemporary schizoid DSM nomenclature (an attitude of "need no one – aware of no one") to those schizoids seemingly interpersonally avoidant. Fairbairn noted that the typical characterization of the schizoid is slightly deceptive as many schizoids (called "secret schizoids" by Ralph Klein) seem socially available and engaged. Here Fairbairn included schizoid "exhibitionism" and schizoid "role-playing." Both psychological techniques are ways to *show* the self while still not *giving* of the self, protecting the self from any appropriation. Building on Fairbairn's astute clinical observations Harry Guntrip, Fairbairn's famous analysand, organized the schizoid into the following *traits*:[2]

(a) *Introversion* in which all libidinal strivings remain principally directed toward internal object relations; this is often, but not necessarily, accompanied by a rich and varied phantasy/imaginative life as, for the schizoid, an inner life is experienced as a sanctuary to outer relations.
(b) *Withdrawnness or an essential detachment*, overt or covert, which is mainly experienced by others as a reluctance to or avoidance of entering into the interpersonal domain from an emotional point of view as evident in the patient description above.
(c) *Narcissism and self-sufficiency* as cooperation or "doing-with-others" evoke fears of dependency and appropriation.

(d) *A sense of superiority* or standing apart and above others *rather* than the need for fusion of mirroring of grandiosity as seen in narcissism.
(e) *Loss of affect*, which is the by-product of defensive inwardness, is behaviorally observed as a fundamental attitude of cynicism, general aloofness, and lack of interpersonal empathy. For the schizoid to *feel* is to *connect* and to connect is to be appropriated.
(f) *Extreme loneliness* that can be ascribed to excessive self-sufficiency and superiority (as safety mechanisms) resulting in a deep longing which paradoxically brings their central fear of appropriation back into focus.
(g) *Depersonalization* as a dissociative defense reflecting an experience of loss of a sense of individuality and identity – an unbearable anxiety for most schizoid individuals.
(h) *Regression* as a dual-track defense and need – that of moving "inward" and "backward." The continual search for enclosures, enclaves, and other womb-like experiences is central to the schizoid's adaptation and feeling of safety.

The Split Internal World of the Schizoid[3]

Based on the work of Fairbairn, Guntrip, and Masterson, Ralph Klein conceptualized a split intrapsychic paradigm[4] based on two separate but interrelated "units" – each with its unique self-representation, object representation, and linking affect (see figure below). The units are described as the master/slave (attachment) and the sadistic object/self-in-exile (nonattachment) units. Considering the master/slave part unit, the object representation is one of a maternal part-object that is both experienced and internalized as coercive if not appropriating, that is, a master that only wants to "use" and "direct" the person. The part-self representation is one of an enslaved self who provides a function. The central affect linking the part representations is being jailed but connected and the relief of not being alienated. Klein describes a classic case of such:

> (Like) a puppet on a ventriloquist's knee…I was trapped…unable to move or act except as she commanded me to do. I had a mind of my own, but it made no difference. No one cared, and no one asked. I simply mouthed the words that she wanted and expected to

> hear. And if I didn't submit, I felt I would be discarded. Put aside. I would be away from her control, but I would be alone, exiled. To stay connected I had to be her slave.
>
> (Klein, in Masterson and Klein 1995, p. 62)

Schizoids also frequently describe themselves as being "too much" (the "death" of mother/others), an irritant, unseen but needed, and "just there."

For the sadistic object/self-in-exile part unit, the object representation is of a maternal part-object which is experienced and internalized as sadistic, dangerous, depriving, and even abandoning in relationship to a part-self-representation of being alienated, in exile. Despite being exiled, the experience is one of being self-contained and self-reliant. The primary affects of the abandonment depression are despair,[5] desuetude, rage, loneliness, and fear of cosmic aloneness (void):

> What is meant to be conveyed by the designation of the object representation as the master? A schizoid patient who makes an effort at relatedness (in the internal world or external reality) is likely to experience the object as being manipulating, coercive, and appropriating. The object is enslaving and imprisoning...Attachment is perceived as hazardous to the schizoid's health. The quality of attachment can only marginally be characterized as emotionally gratifying and sustaining; it seems to fulfill only the most basic needs associated with relatedness. At times it may only function to *exert the gravitational force necessary to keep the schizoid patient from hurtling beyond the point of no return.*
>
> (Klein, in Masterson and Klein 1995, pp. 59–60) (italics added)

Furthermore, according to Klein,

> 'Home' for the schizoid patient is the nonattachment unit. Such patients usually 'live' within the sadistic/self-in-exile unit...For schizoid patients, the self-in-exile is the place where they have to go and that will always take them in safely. Whereas patients with other disorders of self are constantly struggling to live within their attachment experiences (the RORU or the omnipotent object/grandiose self unit), the schizoid patient's first and primary concern is to

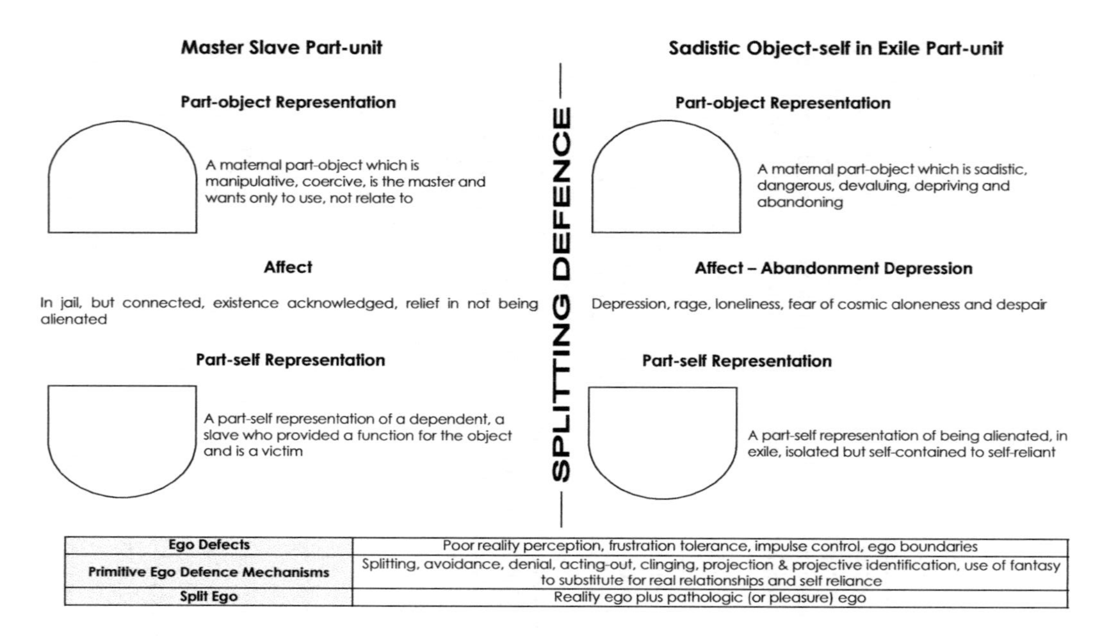

Ego Defects	Poor reality perception, frustration tolerance, impulse control, ego boundaries
Primitive Ego Defence Mechanisms	Splitting, avoidance, denial, acting-out, clinging, projection & projective identification, use of fantasy to substitute for real relationships and self reliance
Split Ego	Reality ego plus pathologic (or pleasure) ego

Figure 5.1 Split Objects Relations Unit of the Schizoid Disorder of Self.

> stabilize and secure his or her existence within the sadistic object/self-in–exile unit.
>
> (1995, p. 52)

An analysand of the author described it as such:

> I think she (mother) hated me, she could not get herself to say it but her behavior towards me betrayed it. I was an irritant to her...I was untouched by her hate of me. I would recite poetry in my head, even at times sing inside. I was everywhere except with her. That is what kept me sane. I had to learn to totally separate myself from her and just do if she commanded it (slave), and when I did wrong, which was always, I went into myself as a way to keep her at bay (exile)...I live very orbitally still.

According to Klein and Masterson, and in agreement with both Fairbairn and Guntrip, the schizoid client may also take on various behavioral patterns, seeing variation in clinical presentations. Pearson (2004, p. 45) summarizes the *schizoid clusters* as follows:

1. The *pure schizoid cluster*, which consists mainly of withdrawal, introversion, and lack of affect.
2. The *narcissistic cluster*, which consists mainly of narcissism, superiority, and self-reliance.
3. The *borderline cluster*, which consists mainly of depersonalization, regression, and loneliness.

Although seemingly complicated, dream material frequently supports the analysand and the therapist in differentiating the schizoid clusters. Concerning the pure schizoid, as described in the case study of Paul[6] (Daws, 2009), the very need to attach activates defenses, or in the thinking of Hedges (1997, p. 114), "Contact itself is the feared element because it brings a promise of love, safety, and comfort that cannot be fulfilled and that reminds [the patient] of the abrupt breaches of infancy." In Paul's dreams, one is made acutely aware of how need and communion (eating), being social (the bar), using one's own image (narcissism-reflection in water) can activate sadistic objects (internal saboteurs), and self-in-exile needs (Daws, 2009, pp. 32–33):

> *Dream 1*: My girlfriend and I were cooking and just spending time together…suddenly a group of armed men stormed into the kitchen and started to shoot at us…we try to get away.
> *Dream 2*: We are walking with a bunch of people on a path when suddenly, someone starts shooting at us…I jump into one of the bushes as my fiancée runs off with the others to take cover. I can see the assassin sitting on a ridge, and I start to circle to catch him.
> *Dream 3*: I am sitting in a bar, and there are people sitting close to the wall at various tables, drinking and enjoying themselves. Suddenly an assassin shoots through the wall and kills all the people. After the killing, people come in and clean the bar, fix the wall, and new people arrive at the scene…they sit, and it happens again…I try to warn them, but nothing stops the people from coming and sitting again…I then dreamt that I was alone at a peaceful house next to the sea [schizoid withdrawal?].
> *Dream 4*: Two people and I are hunting a serial killer in a forest. The two go off by themselves, and I am left alone. I start looking for the killer. I become aware that I am thirsty, I see a lake and go to drink water. As I bend over to drink, I see the serial killer behind me. He grabs me around the neck and tries to cut my throat. I wondered where the others are… (looking dissociated).

The associations that followed were also of interest (Daws, 2009, pp. 33–34):

Paul: I don't know what it means…I wish that I could be like a computer…My thoughts are mine…I am pre-occupied with having original thoughts…Thoughts that are not the result or product of someone else…Do you think people ever have their own thoughts or are we just reacting upon what is given to us… (becoming melancholic). You know it is like in a sci-fi book that I read – a ball that sucks in everything…it spins. As it spins, it sucks up everything but stays the same size…it goes to the earth's core and sucks the earth in…It sucks in everything [love turned hungry, hunger is dangerous]. Still, it stays the same size…strange.

Paul also described his life as "a windmill in a desert," reflecting loneliness and a secret connection to a deeper source, similar to the "sucking ball." The very need for closeness and the fear it entails creates a unique dilemma, referred to by Guntrip as the "in and out program." The compromise can be viewed as a sort of halfway house position, neither allowing for the possibility of appropriation nor needing to feel cut off. The flow evident in the schizoid process is referred to by Masterson as the *Schizoid Triad* and is explained as follows,

> In the case of the schizoid, as Masterson and Klein view it, the movement toward the self is exhibited as an attempt at experiencing feelings, closeness, or spontaneity, and is followed by dysphoric affect that is predominantly fear of being attacked or swallowed up, but is also a fear of harming or offending the object and causing it to withdraw. Both fears exist simultaneously. The defense is almost always distancing, sometimes including withdrawal into fantasies of intimacy.
>
> (Manfield, 1992, p. 221)

This seems evident in Paul's dreams. Closeness, oral derivatives of need (kitchen, bar), spending time together, being social, and even having one's own need (thirst) met finds the activation of the anti-libidinal, the anti-need parts of the personality. In Dream 4, we could later identify the pattern to be his anti-libidinal twin (reflection in the water, seeing the serial killer) that is evoked when he experiences need. Memories soon surfaced, linking his mother and father to critical attitudes concerning his needs and wants. The envious sadistic, and destructive self-object unit became evident in various interpersonal scenarios and always had the same effect – shooting, ambushing the other, and his self-needs. From Dreams 1, 2, and 3, I frequently wondered if the internal saboteur was not evoked during an experience of *unguarded neediness* for not only intimate but even social relationships.

The free association[7] that followed the dreams does, however, reflect Paul's deep underlying schizoid adaptation with his fear of love and need turned hungry (kitchen scenario), being attacked by the narcissistic and envious internal saboteur when needs are enacted upon (while drinking), and finally, that needs are experienced as inherently destructive, i.e., devouring and destroying (devouring mother earth). Paul's schizoid anxieties plagued his relationships, making it impossible to allow closeness. I may even serve as a reason for his lack of physical hunger (no-mouth):

> Introjection (sucking in the dream) is in itself a schizoid withdrawal from external object relations in real life, and is the chief agent in creating the *inner dream world* which Fairbairn regards as a universal schizoid phenomenon based on fundamental splitting of the ego.
>
> (Guntrip, 1969, p. 299)

The "sucking-in," for Guntrip, can be explained as the identification with the mother and is experienced to be both the mother swallowing the infant and the infant swallowing the mother – a mutual swallowing and a mutual merger. Identification implies, paradoxically, the loss of self.

Pseudo Borderline Cluster – Samantha, the Witch, and Entombment

Samantha consulted the author with feelings of ennui. Samantha has lived alone for most of her adult life and has one adult son. A theatrical, enticing, and engulfing mother eclipsed her developmental history, and Samantha's central role in the family was to function as the moderator. Samantha struggled to free herself from overwhelming feelings of melancholia and indescribable loneliness. Uncertain at times if much of Samantha's adaptation could be ascribed to a hysteroid transformation, the following dreams supported a deeper understanding of the pseudo-borderline schizoid structure:

Samantha: I am at a theme park – it's bustling and lively [looking enlivened] – there is food… and a witch! [food and need activate the bad object] Frightening [joy to fear]. Then I became aware that just beside the theme park, a concentration camp is located (starts crying) – a fence with prisoners standing in the mud – they are emaciated, with vacant eyes, and hungry. I want to help them (crying). [moving to the right side of the split units]

After adapting to a schizoid understanding and interventions, Samantha also dreamt about both the sadistic object, self-in-exile, and the slave position in greater emotional clarity: " I am in a room. I can see a Nazi-looking doctor [sadistic object], as well as my son. I have to go into a suspended animation tank. I know I have no choice. I am both saddened and relieved." Exploration uncovered being with others (myself and being a mother) implied being commanded, controlled (concentration camp), and committed (motherhood and love as enslavement). The suspended animation tank served as a painful symbol of the entombment of the true self, given her developmental history and experience with relationships.

Pseudo Narcissistic Schizoid – Mr. Agent Man

Simon, a tall, knowledgeable, and distinguished-looking engineer, consulted me after his live-in partner grew impatient with his indecisiveness (to get married), extreme self-preoccupation (which they labeled narcissistic), and somewhat distant demeanor. They had been living together for 10 years, with the understanding that marriage was an empty Western ritual. On the one hand, Simon adored and cared for his partner but ultimately felt betrayed by her change of heart and was increasingly resentful of her continual pressure to marry. Therapeutically I found it challenging to engage with Simon as I felt kept at a respectful distance, subtly maneuverer to stay on his train of thought (I the enslaved person and he the master?). It would not be challenging to interpret Simon's approach to life and behavior as rather self-involved and self-centered, although his presencing seemed more observational, removed, and "from above." I decided on safety comments and was rewarded by Simon bringing dreams of being an agent, always on the run, hiding in unseen places to "monitor" his pursuers. During the third session, he shared the following dreams and associations:

Simon: I had a dream. I was with a bunch of people, and I was not sure what I was doing there. Were we anthropologists? (theme of observing culture) On the one side was a massive pot with primitive people – they were cooking the people they caught! This reminds me, Loray – do you know the difference between commitment and dedication? Well, a chicken is dedicated as it lays eggs for its masters daily, but a pig is committed as it is fed only to be eaten!

Dreams 2 and 3 [following *giving in* and deciding to get married]. I had a most frustrating dream – I was flying, but not high; something was controlling me. I was flying a few meters above the ground. I could go left and right but not up or down – something holding me there. And then the other dream bothered me.[8] I was a spy, and I

> got caught by a mobster. Serious looking guy. He took me to a big white car, and the trunk was open – I knew what that meant – if I did not join him, he would kill me and dump me somewhere. I knew I had no choice – join him and live, but become a mobster – or say no and end up in a trunk – killed.

Given the gifts of the dreams shared, Simon started the process of understanding his closed internal world and the various projections of the split object relations units onto the environment, most notably, his soon-to-be wife. Simon valiantly struggled with the fears of being controlled, appropriated, and subsumed by the possibility of "union," i.e., "marriage." Irrespective of the various subtypes of schizoid dilemmas and symptomatology, the schizoid patient experiences a specific, stable, and entrenched internal split. It is this very split that needs to be held and therapeutically addressed.

Psychoanalytic Therapy of the Schizoid Dilemma and the Goldilocks Principle – The Need for Safety and the Importance of Environmental Transference

The therapeutic attitude needed to sustain meaningful contact with the schizoid analysand without being either intrusive-controlling or distant-disinterested can prove challenging. By definition, the duration of the therapy (shorter-term and longer-term) will also influence the choice of intervention. Nonetheless, whereas the borderline dilemmas respond to clarification and confrontation and narcissistic clients respond well to the interpretation of narcissistic vulnerability (pain, self-defense) (Daws, 2013), the schizoid client is found to respond optimally when invited to partake in the psychotherapeutic dialogue through the use of *consensus matching* within which the interpretation of the *schizoid dilemma and compromise* can be addressed.[9] *Transitional language*, and what I refer to as the "Goldilocks principle," is relied upon to ensure a natural measure of *interpersonal safety through affective and cognitive approximation.* Thoughts from the therapist, as notes to the other, ultimately serve as possibilities to be contemplated without demand ("I was thinking," "I wonder about x and let me know if I got it right," etc.) supporting the schizoid to find the "just right" measure of interpersonal distance, thought and feeling as *experienced and found by them.*

To reiterate, the interpretation of the schizoid dilemma remains the primary intervention and is described by Klein as follows: "The schizoid dilemma is that the patient can be neither too close nor too far in emotional distance from another person without experiencing conflict and anxiety" (Klein, in Masterson et al., 1995, p. 44). A clinical example from the Mastersonian Jerry Katz illustrates the use of transitional language, the Goldilocks principle, and the schizoid dilemma:

> I had a thought about how you might experience being in the room with me. I would be curious to know if this makes sense to you. It seems to me that being too close or too far from me may pose a dilemma for you. Acting on a wish to have connection with me might leave you open to feeling rejected or coerced or manipulated by me – sort of like a slave who has to do what I want or else have nothing – yet, on the other hand, keeping yourself at too great a distance might leave you feeling profoundly isolated and cut off.
>
> (Katz, in Masterson et al., 2004, p. 102)

Klein also introduced a second critical intervention – that of the *schizoid compromise*. After the long work of establishing a therapeutic alliance, the patient is expected to face the painful challenge of the abandonment depression, "Here the therapist must look for all signs of defense and resistance and interpret the patient's willingness to 'settle' or 'compromise' on a relatively safe and comfortable distance without working through the abandonment depression" (Klein, in Masterson et al., 1995, p. 44). It can be said that the compromise may be a behavior, thought pattern, or relational approach (Katz, 2004). By interpreting the various compromises, the analysand may see how they actively, although certainly unconsciously, create distance and find that interpersonal negotiation and closeness may be an option (without its various projected fears). Indeed, the higher functioning the schizoid analysand, the more comfortable the analyst can address relational difficulties directly. It is crucial to remain aware that the schizoid analysand may easily comply with the needs of analysis (slave position) or partake in highly intellectual debates, making them seem very involved but without much affective change. The latter remains an analytic challenge, needing prudent clinical judgment and intervention.

Finally, to support the listening process and interpretation strategies of the schizoid dilemma and compromise, Masterson's unique algorithm (referred to as the "schizoid triad") may also orientate the clinician within the session. As mentioned in previous chapters, whereas the borderline triad can be summarized as self-activation (separation-individuation) leads to anxiety that leads to defense, and the narcissistic triad as imperfection leads to anxiety that leads to defense, the schizoid triad can be summarized as closeness/contact leads to anxiety that leads to defense. An example:

> John, as you were relating this conflict with your wife, I became aware of your difficulty. Let me know your thoughts on it. I notice that when you have a good day with your wife, you mention you start to feel closed in, suffocated, her wanting too much, and then you retreat into a silence that she grows angry with. I wonder if a good day with her does not create anxiety about being close, maybe too close, and by retreating into silence and your office, you try to create a safer distance from her, your anxiety, and the growing intimacy between the two of you.

Being with the Schizoid Dilemma Therapeutically – The Case of Thea[10]

Thea, who is in her early 60s, was referred for treatment for depression. She was the firstborn of two children and described her mother as a fragile woman who gave birth young to a daughter who overwhelmed her. Thea was often told tales of how she was a very difficult infant who could not be soothed and cried incessantly. Thea's father was unfaithful to her mother during her mother's pregnancy, something Thea discovered with horror as an adult. As Thea developed, and especially following the birth of her younger sibling, Thea became closer to her father. This was to have a deleterious consequence after the parental marriage ended, as her father refused to have any further contact with his now-adult children. Thea found this loss agonizing. Thea's own marriage also ended painfully when her husband left after a decade without warning.

Thea has a son to whom she is greatly attached. His immigration, as expected, produced a rather painful and protracted depression. Although Thea's son and wife had invited her to live with them, Thea had been reluctant to do so, feeling she would be a significant imposition and that a sense of obligation would trap her.

Thea has a strong and abiding faith, a powerful organizing principle in her life. As a result of her strong beliefs, Thea has been involved in a faith-based community, heading up an agency concerned with the welfare of its community members. Although Thea is attractive, with a kind and empathic personality, she has had no significant romantic attachments since her divorce. She prefers to devote her life to her chosen profession and her agency work. Being devout presented Thea with various dilemmas and complex feelings. Thea mentions that although she wanted a "quiet life," she had to put her needs and desires aside, seeing her having to be "a big girl." In most doings, Thea mentions that she can feel safe in the notion that "God's in charge." Thea sometimes feels "a great deal of resentment, anger even," given the church and agency's reluctance to remunerate her fairly. Moreover, the lack of recognition of Thea's efforts has had an impact of its own, "I had been slaving, slaving (laughs) for a month to get things ready," and her colleagues saw it as a "piece of cake," minimizing her input.

Analyst: "I wonder if that reminds you of the dilemma of knowing what you should receive and yet not daring to complain if you don't get it, which leaves you feeling that it's such a struggle to fight for your necessities and your survival."

Thea: " Yes, and I don't understand why they don't familiarize themselves with what is due to me, and I'm the one that has to make sure I get what's due to me."

Analyst: "If you ask for what is due to you, you will be perceived as being greedy. It's almost as though you were saying: I have needs, and this is normal, but if you don't recognize my needs, then I'm stuck in a place where if you say you have those needs, you're bad, but if you don't say you do, then nobody notices."

Thea: "It feels like a rejection of me."

Thea copes by reminding herself to be an "adult and just suck it up"; "I've chosen where I am. It's not like I'm in prison or anything." *A true* dilemma! She has faced it all her life, bringing to my mind an infant deprived too soon. Thea is constantly haunted that "there is a part of me that will do something really terrible," and when she isn't supported in her decisions at work, she worries, "Did I do something terrible?" As a result of this primal dilemma, Thea decided early in her life to manage her innate needs and desires in a way that would not destroy her mother by splitting off the needy parts of her that caused her such life-threatening terror as an infant. Still, these continued to generate intense anxiety, birthing a part that would inexorably negotiate survival in the world at the cost of her Real Self, creativity, spontaneity, and joy, "I think I'm that kind of person that I feel I'm alone but I probably make myself alone." Even when turning down an invitation, Thea would think, "Gee, I wish I could be with them, but actually, it's…too much effort. I prefer to be on my own." Thea's preference to be on her own, although indicating a sense of independence and resourcefulness, also contained a deeper painful self-experience, "I don't believe I am entitled to ask for anything. That's why I've always tried to be independent." And yet, Thea also longs to have a partner on whom she can depend, "I do long for that. I can't imagine what it would be like, but it feels so very scary, so I run away from even just the thought of having another man in my life – ever."

Thea's way of relating manifested in her belief that she should be self-contained even with me.

Analyst: "I wonder if it feels to you that to be in a relationship here with me might also feel as though you owe me something [Masters-slave unit]"

Thea: "I pay you, and I don't have to feel that I owe you anything. It is a relief; otherwise, it would have been a terrible burden on me … I'd hate to overwhelm you, so maybe I do edit out parts of me, except I don't know what I do edit out because I don't know how I really am."

Analyst: "I wonder what it would be like for you to come and cry in here even – you've so seldom cried, and I was thinking that perhaps it is your fear that I, too, would be overwhelmed by your crying."

Thea: "Yes, I would think that: When I've been on my own, I've cried. You know, I've really sobbed, but then afterward, I think, where is this getting me? So I just stop."

Analyst: "It was almost as though you'd never had an experience in your life of being comforted or consoled. What would be the difference between crying on your own or in my presence?"

Thea: [She reflected that this is a constant dilemma] "I don't know what to say without hurting [others'] feelings. They'll leave me if I make myself vulnerable to wanting to be loved. They won't understand that if I love them, I need them. But yet, I understand

> that because I love them, it doesn't mean they owe me their life. I have needs, I suppose, and I would like them to be met. I don't know how...how...far my needs should be met and whether I'm being unreasonable with my needs, and I don't know, and maybe sometimes I test it, and they don't get met, so I reduce my needs."

This was such a clear exposition of Thea's schizoid dilemma: Thea would negate her needs and respond to the needs of others, which left her depleted, used, and even rage-filled at times. The latter reactivated Thea's retreat into exile where she could be safe, if alone and alienated, seeing herself as "not normal," a common refrain. Given the schizoid dilemma, the therapeutic process over time gave understanding to the countertransferential fear that contact could overwhelm Thea. In retrospect, such a fear could be interpreted as the countertransferential projective identification of the sadistic object relations unit. Thea would frequently talk at length, inducing a feeling of a *chase,* if not a fruitless pursuit. Thea was also very wary of therapy, preferring to engage in matters with a practical view to finding a solution than to engage in a therapeutic alliance. Thea was also initially averse to meeting weekly for therapy, dismissing her need for treatment at all, seeing herself as weak when comparing herself to others she believed suffered more significant adversity. It appeared that allowing herself to want a connection with me caused distress. However, after about two years, Thea settled into more regular attendance, about which she continued to feel some ambivalence. And yet, gradually, the therapeutic relationship deepened, and goodbyes were exchanged with genuine affection and warmth when therapy ended.

At the beginning of the therapy, it was also clear that Thea didn't wish to verbalize matters pertaining to her inner life. I would also struggle to connect at times, almost feeling like an outsider visiting a foreign land. Again, what an interesting and secret glimpse through countertransference of the alienated anti-libidinal part unit. Only after some years did Thea begin to link her inner states to her behaviors and the lack of emotional intimacy in her relationships. She explained that "if someone is nice to me, I feel I owe them, and I don't want to be in that relationship because I'd have to repay that." And again, fearing perhaps she doesn't have the right to even exist, "I suppose either that I owe – I might not be able to put into words exactly who I owe, and that but...I feel I owe, I owe for the right to be here." "Being loved is a burden," one she doesn't "know how to repay. I don't know what's expected of me. (Sighs) and then I start thinking, 'am I serving the way I should?'" Not surprisingly, she "usually get[s] very tense about people invading [her] space." Worse yet than being in exile can be Thea's various experiences of being in relationships, which she describes as hurtful, stabbing, piercing, being stoned, i.e., having stones thrown at her, things blowing up, being mocked, being and feeling defenseless, with no guard, being hung out to dry, and being "broken" by others [sadistic object relations unit]. Even so, Thea believes, "everyone in my life leaves me, and that proves…[how] I am [abandonment derivative]. "It must be me because it happens so often I must be the one blowing things up." This essential struggle leaves Thea with a rage that cannot be expressed. Even when Thea is legitimately angry and wishes to express her disappointment, she avoids it, worrying that she could be, "destroying" the other. Over and over, "I allow myself to feel guilty, and if I don't then I feel terrible because I feel I'm hard, you know" (almost as though this is a universal rule).

Thea also remembers her mother as follows, "I think she…she was just out of her depth and didn't know what to do. I … feel that the more enraged I became, the more out of her depth she became." Consequently, her mother would "tip-toe around [her] as though she would explode." Later, Thea explained, "My mom was afraid of me. Not that I would hurt her, but just that she was in awe of me…not like in awe of like 'she's the most fantastic creature in the world', but more in awe that I'd explode." She spoke with sadness of how her mom, "all her life…would say to me…I'm not normal. I knew what that meant for her." In this way, Thea became the sadistic one of the relationship, fearing her power to destroy, seeing herself as the "crazy, stuck person" to have a (depleted, unsatisfactory) relationship rather than hold any animosity toward her mother, "I did feel there was something about me that made my mother not cope. I think I might have destroyed her." To this, I wondered aloud if it could be terrifying for a baby when a mother cannot cope. Thea agreed that, "by rescuing the mom, the baby rescues itself. I cannot 'not' rescue her because I won't survive."

Thea greatly admires animals as they don't have to worry and "take it for granted that they have a right to be here. That must be wonderful." It took time to verbalize her desire to know she's "not taking up anybody else's space [nor] infringing on anyone's human rights.

[That] this space here, my body and everything is my space, and I don't owe anyone anything for it," to which I responded, "that sounds like a mission statement," and she agreed chuckling, "yeah, my mission statement." Such episodes of *communicative matching* became more frequent. On one occasion, when two colleagues came to blows, we bantered about the absurdity of their conflict, and when they ended up in her office, one accused her, saying it was her fault. At which point she laughed. "Your fault!" I exclaimed, and we both laughed (uproariously).

It was a relief for Thea to begin to try different behaviors, thoughts, and feelings (self-activate),"Maybe I can try to practice giving myself some space so that it doesn't overwhelm me...So now I'm getting more immune (laughs) it's a good thing." She also realized when going to see the psychiatrist that far from asking for more medication, "I don't think I will. I'm feeling stronger now." And most touchingly, she celebrated how "I used to want to be alone, and I wanted to die alone. But I don't now. I want to be with those who love me and whom I love. And to know I won't die alone."

Countertransference Difficulties in Holding the Defensive Self of the Schizoid Analysand

As evident in the case studies presented, the analyst working within the schizoid dilemma may become the recipient of, or resonate with, the projected part-self or part-object relations units on both sides of the split. That is, the interpersonal demands of the analytic process may see the analyst experiencing, for example, being enslaved, the enslaver (the master), the sadistic controlling other (exiler), or being exiled in the therapeutic hour. In creative tandem, this could provide important information about the SR or OR of the analysand and be held and explored based on the therapeutic need of the analysand, their ego-capacities, and the stage of therapy. A typical countertransferential response and experience of analysts working with schizoid analysands is one of being exiled. The need for meaningful therapeutic contact may give rise to impinging and invasive interpretations, paradoxically stimulating, in many, a slave position. As mentioned, various permutations are possible and need to be carefully tracked and explored to see if the process can support working through.

Notes

1 See also Winnicott's work entitled *Human Nature*, section III (Establishment of Unit Status), Chapters 4 and 5, *The Earliest States* and *A Primary State of Being: Pre-Primitive States* (pp. 126–134). Impingement is visually articulated with great effect!

2 Also review Guntrip, 1969, Part 1, Chapters 1–3, *Clinical Descriptions of the Schizoid Personality*, as well as Part 3, Chapters 6–9, *The Nature of Basic Ego-Weakness*.

3 Fairbairn's 1944 structural theory emerged from a detailed analysis of a patient's dream (see Fairbairn, 1952, pp. 95–106). In analyzing the dream from an object relations perspective, i.e., that for every self-structure, there is an object structure with linking affect, Fairbairn noted that the patient had *separate* views of herself and her significant others. The following pairs of structures were observed by Fairbairn and can be read in more detail in the upcoming book of Celani in this series:

   (a) The Central Ego and its relationship with the Ideal Object (the "good or nurturing object" other). This structure is largely conscious.
   (b) The Anti-libidinal Ego that is largely unconscious and contains an internal self-representation of the largely neglected, humiliated, and enraged child in a relationship with the Rejecting Object, which is an internal representation of an abusive and neglecting parent.
   (c) The second unconscious pair is the Libidinal Ego which is the child's fantasy of the good loving parent whom he longs if not pines for in relationship to the Exciting Object, which is a phantasized representation of a loving and devoted parent that offers hope.
   (d) Working with traumatized soldiers and abused children, Fairbairn recognized the painful endopsychic reality that the need for connection and love remains so powerful that the child creates, similar to Harlow's monkeys, a good parent out of minimal parental investment. Given the anti-libidinal ego, the aim of the libidinal self is clear – to reform the rejecting objects and to know its wants and needs so as to ensure contact and love (the latter is called the attachment to the Bad Object).

4 The sophisticated reader and clinician are referred here to Dr. Orcutt's revisioning of the schizoid split object relations units in her work *The Unanswered Self* (2021), Chapter 6, The Diagrams, especially page 161 with diagram 6.1 wherein Dr. Orcutt successfully argues an alternative diagram depicting hatching difficulty. The discussion is furthered in Chapter 7, wherein self-states are thoroughly discussed as related to Masterson, trauma, and dissociation.

5 Also see the work of James Hollis, *Swamplands of the Soul: New Life in Dismal Places* (1996). In this transformative and rather brilliant conceptualization, Hollis discusses, in Chapter 4, the main psychological

differences between Depression, Desuetude, and Despair. Many schizoids I have worked with, as desert mothers and fathers, have described experiences very similar to desuetude- children of lost kingdoms, exiled from society.

6 This case was originally published in Daws, L. (2009). Dreaming the dream: In search of endopsychic ontology. *Issues in Psychoanalytic Psychology*, 31(1), 21–40.

7 For Guntrip, "phantasy is primarily a revelation of endopsychic structure" (1969, p. 322).

8 The previous session before the dream he discussed his uncertainty of getting married but 'accepting' the idea that he may have to as not doing so may lead to him losing her.

9 I am indebted to Dr. Orcutt for making me aware that the schizoid compromise was first described by Harry Guntrip in his 1969 work.

10 Thank you, Dr. Anne-Marie Lydall, and your analysand for the description.

Part 4

Distinction

Separation Individuation in the Practicing Subphase of Development – the Narcissistic Dilemma and Separation Individuation in the Rapprochement Subphase of Development – the Borderline Dilemma

Chapter 6

The Tyranny of Fusion and Omnipotence

The Narcissistic Dilemma

Introduction

Healthy narcissism, its developmental necessity, and its various creative functions have largely been overshadowed by its malignant transformations frequently encountered in the clinical and cultural setting. Therapeutic approaches to narcissism have received detailed attention from various psychoanalytic scholars, most notably Drs. Otto Kernberg (1975) and Heinz Kohut (1971). Reviewing the work of Masterson (1976, 1993, 2004) and Klein (in Detrick & Detrick, 1989), the reader finds various debates concerning the overlap and differences between the various analysts and their unique clinical view of narcissism's impact; that is, its beneficial qualities (self-object needs), its malignant qualities (psychopathy, malignant narcissism), and its relation to fusional complexes (false self-adaptation). Masterson's thinking will now be explored in greater depth.

Masterson's Developmental Self and Object Relations Approach to Narcissism

As reviewed in Chapter 2, the toddler gradually awakens to a unique developmental paradox during the practicing subphase of development. Being part of a protective union and acquiring up-right locomotion activates a powerful surge of libidinal capacity and supplies. For Mahler, this surge is evident in the toddler's love affair with the world, explorative behavior, inexhaustible curiosity, and imperviousness to bumps and falls.[1] Despite the love affair with the world and its intoxicating spell, the world of natural values is expected to progressively dawn upon the unsuspecting toddler, at times with much surprise and

DOI: 10.4324/9781003358572-10

despair. Limits are also soon felt, both physically and psychologically, and no preventative approaches of the mother or environment will protect the toddler from such deflation, if not disillusionment. During this phase of immense psychological development, an emotionally attuned and responsive mother remains essential. Maternal attunement navigates exploration needs, manages the complex affective domains of inflation-deflation on self and object representations, and sets sensitive limits while enjoying and taking pride in the toddler's growing abilities and expanding personality (authentic self-idiom). For Masterson, the mothering other's central attitude (and thus behavior) is one of psychological midwife, bridging the painful developmental process of much-needed omnipotence to a more significant reality-orientated adjustment. It is expected that such midwifery would ensure the following:

A) The progressive differentiation of self *from* the object.
B) The progressive differentiation of self *and* object.
C) The progressive defusing of infantile omnipotence while libidinizing needed ego functions linked to mastering tasks in reality (and general learning), thereby supporting the internalization of cause and effect, i.e., the world of natural laws. The latter supports the notion that healthy self-esteem and self-confidence should partner with reality rather than phantasy and omnipotence exclusively.

Despite the progressive and successful defusing of infantile omnipotence, practicing subphase remnants remain reflected in our own private Edens sublimated in intimacy, agency, and creativity. Letting go of infantile omnipotence is an ideal state of mind – the product of years of maturation, practice, failure, and mourning – *even* with a sufficiently attuned mother, father, and environment. According to Masterson's thinking (1993),

> *Healthy narcissism,*[2] *or the real self,* is experienced as a sense of self that feels adequate and competent, a feeling derived mostly from reality, with some input from phantasy. This sense of self includes appropriate concern for others, and its self-esteem is maintained by the use of self-assertion to master challenges and tasks presented by reality. The intrapsychic structure, which underlies this sense of self, consists of a self-representation that has separated from the

> object representation, has had its infantile grandiosity and omnipotence defused, and is whole – that is, it contains both positive and negative at the same time, and is able to function *autonomously*.
>
> (p. 12) (italics added)

Following Mahler, difficulties in this phase can effectively forestall the rapprochement conflict, finding the toddler, the child, and later the adult caught in the psychological reality of an omnipotent fused unit wherein grandiosity serves as desperate protection against vulnerability and reality considerations. Masterson writes that this illusion is kept intact by various defense mechanisms honed to continuously deny reality (which is painful), keeping the omnipotence intact,

> The fixation of the narcissistic personality disorder must occur *before* this event [rapprochement] because *clinically* the patient behaves *as if* the object representation were an integral part of the self-representation – an omnipotent, dual unity. The possibility of the existence of a rapprochement crisis doesn't seem to dawn on this patient. The fantasy exist that the world is his oyster, he must seal off by avoidance, denial and devaluation those perceptions of reality that do not fit or resonate with this narcissistic, grandiose self-projection. Consequently, he is compelled to suffer the cost to adaptation that is always involved when large segments of reality must be denied.
>
> (Masterson, 1981, pp. 12–13) (italics added)

Masterson provides various possibilities, given his clinical work, for how such a developmental difficulty may arise. One possible explanation is that the mother relies on her child as a narcissistic extension, stimulating the child's grandiosity at the expense of reality considerations and limitations:

> No son of mine can *ever* be that inadequate in math. You are as smart as your grandfather (the ultra-successful maternal father). You are going to do great things! Forget what the teacher said – just a teacher. If they were good at math, they wouldn't be teachers, right? Idiots, all of them!

Indeed, given the example, to avoid abandonment and devaluation, the child has no choice but to accept the idealizing tendencies and needs of the mother, compelled to comply with the projection and demands (idealizing and grandiose): "If I am not perfect, I will be bad and abandoned," *or*, as Ralph Klein writes, "I am perfect (special), but I need you to affirm this (specialness)" (Klein in Detrick & Detrick, 1989, p. 321).

Another developmental pathway is either overtly or subtly rejecting parental attitudes toward the child's natural narcissistic developmental needs and potential, invariably forcing the child to either "bury" his narcissism or, in turn, harbor omnipotent phantasies *secretly* to protect the self against extreme injury, vulnerability, and aloneness. For Klein,

> in this case, the working model of relatedness for the child can be better expressed in the following way; "You are perfect (omnipotent), and I can be part of (share in) your power (specialness)...The child must idealize the object and then feel special by 'basking in the glow' of that object. In this way, the mirroring needs of the child's grandiose self are met, albeit *indirectly*."
>
> (Klein, in Detrick et al., 1989, p. 321)

An example from Masterson: "My Real Self is trapped...My energies have gone to nurture this monster, this clone (false grandiose self), rather than to my real self. I used to have a fantasy as a child of being able to walk on water" (1985, p. 46).

Finally, in the most catastrophic way imaginable, any practicing realities (fusion, inflation, omnipotence, imperviousness, etc.) may be attacked and devalued, that is, and similar to the dream material of the schizoid patient written of above (Paul), all mirroring may evoke a serial killer (the anti-libidinal, the negatively fused aggressive unit), effectively killing off needed narcissistic processes and states! In the concise writing of Lieberman (2004), the following developmental realities with resulting narcissistic style/type are evident:

> When the sense of self of the Narcissistic patient has been so severely injured because of ruptures in any or all of these, a child will:
>
> (1) Dismiss the real self, and try to recapture the narcissistic relationship by becoming grandiose (*manifest/exhibitionistic*).
> (2) Push the real self underground, idealize the object, and try to comply (*closet*).

(3) Or feel under siege, in danger of disintegration or fragmentation if the object was so narcissistically injurious. The child will *give up* being mirrored by, or idealizing, the mother. There is a strong development of the aggressive-empty unit that is projected externally, in order to protect the self against the perception that the other is harsh and attacking (*devaluing*).

(pp. 81–82) (italics added)

For Masterson, thus, the developmental fixation of the narcissist reflects a *split internal world with three developmental possibilities – the manifest/exhibitionistic, the closeted, or the devaluing narcissistic disorder of self.*

The Split Internal World of the Narcissistic Patient

As with the schizoid and borderline disorders of the self, the developmental difficulties faced by the NPD can be understood as a closed intrapsychic system fueled by an intrapsychic split characterized by two fused units. This conceptualization can also be relied upon to understand the variance in narcissistic structures, such as the exhibitionistic, devaluing, and closet narcissistic disorder of the self. The intrapsychic structure (see figure below) of the grandiose (manifest) narcissist consists of a grandiose self-representation and an omnipotent object representation "which have fused into one unit which is more or *less continuously activated*" (Masterson, 1981, p. 29).

This is important as it differs from the schizoid and borderline intrapsychic units, as they reflect more significant differentiation! This may seem counter-intuitive, given the rather chaotic presentation of especially the borderline patient in practice. According to Masterson, the latter can be ascribed to the vacillation *between* the RORU's and WORU's self and object representations (see Chapter 6), whereas, except for the closet narcissist (to be discussed shortly), the manifest narcissist's defenses are continually activated to remain in the left side of the split. Such defensiveness, combined with free access to aggression, coerces the environment to provide mirroring supplies, stabilizing both self-experience and ego functioning with greater success than the borderline disorder of the self. The manifest analysand can then easily appear as

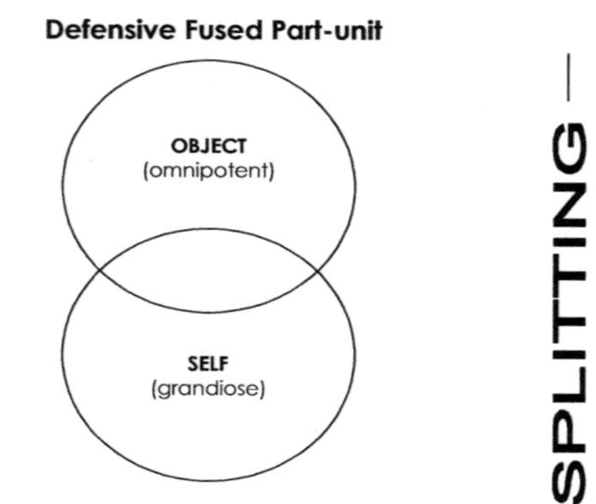

Ego Functions	Poor reality perception, impulse control, frustration tolerance and ego boundaries
Ego Defense Mechanisms	Splitting, avoidance, denial, acting-out, clinging, projection & projective identification

Figure 6.1 Split Object Relations Unit of the Narcissistic Personality Disorder of Self.

"higher" functioning. It must be said that if the analysand does possess various natural gifts, such as attractiveness and other legitimate talents, the differentiation may become even more complex. Many esteem-sensitive individuals possess extraordinary talents and serve their families, work, and communities well. The difficulty arises in how such an analysand functions intrapsychically, interpersonally, and regarding reality considerations. However, for Masterson, the narcissist's false self is more successful than the borderline's false self. As mentioned, this can be ascribed to the *continuous activation of the defensive fused/grandiose unit* defending and protecting against the "underlying aggressive or empty object relations fused unit" (Masterson, 1981, p. 29), and thus the possibility of a painful depression, the feelings of fragmentation (falling apart), or of depletion states. This stands in contrast to the fear of *losing the object* per se, which is separation-sensitive anxiety (a borderline dilemma). A case may elucidate:

> At work I can create applause from moment to moment from my coworkers (narcissistic supplies); however, I expect the same at home from my wife and children. I can recall feeling as a kid I was going to invent a more intricate *airtight entitlement machine* than either of my parents so that I wouldn't feel humiliated and dependent [negative unit] as they seemed to. Entitlements are my self-image [grandiose unit]. Without them I will fall apart and feel alone, humiliated, abandoned, not connected [fragmentation anxiety]. I'm just a big entitlement machine [grandiose unit]...I'm just waiting for magic [practicing subphase fusion], I can't confront the reality that I am on my own. My wife was part of myself. I can't say goodbye. It's the price I pay for having lived in fantasy. It was not worth it unless my entitlements can be magically restored. This can't have happened to me.
>
> (Masterson, 1985, p. 49)

In short, the *defensively fused unit* also supports the linking affects such as being unique, adored, special, perfect, and entitled:

> I want a relationship that is a 100%. Why should I have anything less? When my wife treats me like a hero, I will do anything for her. When she treats me like a hero, I can do anything, conquer anything!

In contrast, the aggressively fused unit can be viewed as the domain of attack, imperfection, shame, and feelings of unworthiness, wherein the impaired self battles immense inadequacy and vulnerability,

> My fall from grace. I was on top of the world and felt nothing could burst my bubble. I had no inkling as to what was to come. I am sure you hear this a lot – an unsuspecting person. This is more than that! I recall so many times like being on a high – a way to not remember not being good enough. My father said I would turn out to be a failure. Worthless.

As so poignantly described by Kohut (1971), the awareness of the right side of the split may be experienced as traumatic to those with narcissistic structures, and great therapeutic care is indicated (Orcutt, 2021).

Diagnostically, Masterson also argued that the various "subtypes" of narcissistic difficulties share a similar intrapsychic split but rely on different defense mechanisms to maintain intrapsychic equilibrium. In treating the *exhibitionistic disorder* of the self (the *inflated false defensive self*), the clinician will, in the beginning stages of the therapy, be principally aware of the defensive/libidinal grandiose self-omnipotent object relations fused unit, that is, a grandiose part object representation that contains power, perfection and so forth, fused with a grandiose part self-representation of being perfect, superior, entitled, with its linking affect of feeling unique, adored, and admired. The manifest/exhibitionistic analysand *projects* this fused unit while underneath, the patient *continuously defends against* the aggressive object relations fused unit that consists of a

> fused object representation that is harsh, punitive, and attacking and a self-representation of being humiliated, attacked, empty, and linked by the affect of the abandonment depression that is experienced more as the *self fragmenting of falling apart* than as the *loss of the object* described by the borderline personality disorder.
>
> (Masterson, 1993, pp. 18–20) (italics added)

An analysand of Orcutt (2021) describes it as follows:

> I'll fight, do anything, not to feel what I feel. I'm putting on a show of how tough I am when I'm falling apart. Nothing holds together if you won't tell me how good I am. Alone, I'm in pieces. I'm

> helpless. I'm a show without an audience, and the stage is falling apart under my feet.
>
> (p. 152)

In contrast to the exhibitionistic disorder, the intrapsychic structure of the closet narcissist differs from the exhibitionistic narcissist in that whereas the exhibitionistic narcissist seems impervious, dismissive, and even callous toward its objects, the closet narcissistic (the *deflated false defensive self*) appears to be both dependent on and even vulnerable to the other. The grandiosity of the self is protected by the projection of the idealized all-good object and then "basking in the glow" of that object; "If I can't see myself reflected positively in the eye of the other person, I have no self" (Lieberman, in Masterson et al., 2004, p. 79). The latter causes greater susceptibility to variance in mood, and closet narcissists thus have greater "access" to dysphoric affect and feelings of depression. When the idealized object fails, the closet narcissist may then project the (activated) internal attacking object onto the external object and, in turn, feel attacked, humiliated, and fragmented, necessitating the search for a new idealized other.

In the traumatic-like case of the devaluing narcissist, the much-needed grandiose self and the idealization of the other seem absent. Instead, what is evident is an active state of *deployment*.[3] According to Lieberman (2004):

> There is no grandiosity of the self or idealization of the other, but the child lives in a stage of siege, with paranoid, schizoid defenses.[4] In treatment, the patient's fragmented self is defended against by projecting either the attacking object or the impaired self onto the therapist. Some of these patients will use the Devaluing defense to maintain a derisive sense of superiority over people in their environments, whereas others will appear to be functioning at a low level, and can often be confused with patients with Schizoid Personality Disorder.
>
> (p. 79)

Thus, the devaluing analysand functions exclusively within the right side of the split – a developmental tragedy and painful state of mind. Pearson (in Masterson et al., 1995, pp. 310–311), conceptualized the devaluing state as protecting the impaired vulnerable self by "discharging and projecting aggression associated with the internalized persecutory and the hungry envious self" through various intrapsychic and interpersonal mechanisms. Pearson's conceptualizations (1995) clearly illustrate the erosive quality of the continual projection of the aggressive unit. An extreme example may suffice. After a clinician showed understanding of an esteem-related dilemma, a severely neglected and shamed analysand, one exposed to continuous verbal attacks, scorn, mocking laughter, and devaluation from her family of origin, responded as follows:

> I see what you are doing! You feel sorry for me as if I am inadequate (impaired self). What makes you so special? [identifying with OR of the negative unit and the aggressor] You think you know what you are talking about, but it sounds like hogwash crap – bullshit psychobabble. Do you think I am an idiot? [reflecting a shift to the SR of the negative unit] YOU are the idiot. You are just saying that crap to soften me up to put me down. Screw you and your superiority, you arrogant s.o.b.

Abandonment Depression and the Narcissistic Dilemma

For the narcissistic analysand, the abandonment depression can be activated or stimulated by true self-activation or by the object's failure to provide the necessary nourishment – *perfect mirroring*. Defenses such as devaluation and splitting can restore the libidinal fused unit, and the "free access" to aggression can also serve as a way to coerce, if not manipulate, the object to mirror perfection, reinstating the grandiose unit of defense. This is especially challenging in malignant narcissists and those with psychopathic tendencies, although esteem trauma may be accessed with time and sensitive intervention. Given the reliance on a *continuously activated* grandiose unit, one can truly begin to grasp the difficulty narcissistic patients will have with depression and human failure! The elements of the abandonment depression experienced by the narcissist are similar to that of the borderline, i.e., suicidal depression, homicidal rage, panic, guilt, hopelessness, helplessness, emptiness, and feelings of void. Clinically, it seems evident that depression is not easily accessed or felt by the exhibitionistic narcissist due to the grandiose defensive structure, whereas the depression experienced by the closet narcissist contains feelings of shame, humiliation, and falling apart. Envy is ever present in narcissistic disorders, as well as feelings of rage. Active avoidance of the experience of depression can be a stumbling block in therapy.

Differential Diagnosis and Treatment

Differentiating the narcissistic patient from the borderline and schizoid patient is central to the Mastersonian Approach. As mentioned by Pearson (in Masterson et al., 2005), understanding the unique language or the "un-narrated self" of the disorders of the self provides the therapeutic frame with a language of regression (borderline), protection against grandiose deflation (narcissism), and the search for safety in compromised contact (schizoid). For Masterson, the borderline intrapsychic structure is developmentally different from the narcissistic intrapsychic structure in that self and object representations are more differentiated and split between rewarding and withholding units that alternate. Narcissistic patients' self and object representations are *fused* and the attachment unit (grandiose unit) is *continuously* activated. According to Masterson (1993):

> The narcissistic style of defense differs from that of the borderline, where the self and object representations are not fused, but separate and split into rewarding and withdrawing part units. The projection of these two part–units are not continuous, but alternate...The borderline patient does not have free access to aggression as does the narcissistic patient. Thus self-assertion, coming up against the withdrawing object projection, is not available for self-esteem. The borderline patient defends by *clinging* to or *distancing* from the object.
>
> (p. 27) (italics added)

Masterson[5] further argues that the projection of the part units is not "airtight," thus lacking the more armored proclivities of the exhibitionistic narcissist. Given the latter, the borderline personality is seen to be more sensitive to reality considerations, "particularly to rewarding and withdrawing responses to self-activation" (1993, p. 27). The latter also creates differences in the transference acting out. The exhibitionistic narcissist seems to be armored by his continuously activated grandiose self, giving the appearance of arrogance and self-centeredness, frequently dismissing the other. The borderline patient vacillates between self-deprecating behavior and irrational anger and/or rage outbursts. Masterson adds that the rage experienced by narcissistic patients is usually experienced as a "cold" rage lacking connectedness. In contrast, the borderline patient's rage is generally centered around intense self-hatred; thus, the therapist may experience greater connectedness.

When considering the idealizing and mirroring projections of the narcissist and the rewarding and withdrawing projections of the borderline, psychoanalytic technique will also have different aims. Firstly, confrontation, the method of choice with the borderline patient, runs the risk of either re-traumatizing the exhibitionist narcissists and/or creating compliance with the closet narcissist. As argued, the continued activation of the fused grandiose self and object representation, with its tendencies toward denial and "air tight" defense against the aggressively self-object unit, leads the patient to experience the confrontation, no matter how well-timed and sensitive, as critique and envious attacks, *activating* the underlying negative unit. For the narcissistic dilemma, the *interpretation of narcissistic vulnerability is central.* The emphasis should instead be on the following sequence:

(a) *Pain*: During this part of the interpretation, the therapist actively identifies and acknowledges the painful affect the patient is experiencing.
(b) *Self*: Focuses on the impact on the patient's self-experience and thus illustrates understanding.
(c) *Defense*: Identify and focus on the defense(s) the patient is using to protect, defend, and soothe the self from the painful affect.

When working with the closeted disorder, further significant therapeutic difficulties arise. To reiterate: The closet narcissist does not seem able to ensure the continuous activation of the grandiose unit, leading to a substantial fluctuation of affect and, thus, greater feelings of inadequacy. The borderline triad, self-activation that leads to depression and defense, is also apparent in the closet narcissist. Finally, as the closet narcissist needs to "bask in the glow" of the idealized other, this behavior can frequently be misread as the clinging defense often found in the borderline dilemma. Given the latter, confrontation would lead to two clinical realities:

(a) Responding with attacks and devaluation with "you do not understand me," or
(b) Compliance, but with no change in affect.

Lastly, many clinicians rightly observe that various schizoids may, at times, appear narcissistic. The narcissism displayed by the schizoid personality should be understood as the schizoid patient's need for *safety through superiority*. Succinctly stated, by acting *above* others, the schizoid can feel safe and self-sufficient, and it is not the result of an underlying grandiose self-representation in need of perfect mirroring (or basking in the glow of the idealized other). Fusion for the schizoid equals appropriation! The unfolding psychotherapeutic process is sometimes the only avenue to distinguish between the latter realities

Therapeutic Work with the Narcissistic Disorders of Self – Jim and the Closet Dilemma

The following are synoptic therapeutic moments of interventions from a psychotherapeutic process with an individual diagnosed with a closet narcissistic disorder of the self. Interventions would include empathically making the patient aware of their vulnerability to experiencing emotional hurt, being injured, feeling fragmented, or feeling small and insignificant. In other words, the analyst and analysand progressively gain insight into the fragile self's intrapsychic dilemmas in a non-shaming manner *together*. This is important as individuals would have different tolerance levels for "separate"-mindedness and may assume, or expect, fusion.

After five years of once-a-week psychodynamic psychotherapy, Jim started expressing that he has realized that what he needs from his analyst is to be the *same as him*. This way, Jim mused, he could feel that whatever badness he may possess would be acceptable, as he is like me, his analyst, who is good and acceptable. As would be expected from the closet narcissistic intrapsychic dilemma, Jim has primarily been idealizing his analyst. Jim has also learned that his analyst is married with children and thoroughly believes that his analyst is a good father and husband, something to *aspire* to. Jim's mother also influenced his idealization tendencies and aspirational needs, and given the closeted conflict, Jim wholeheartedly resonated with her definition of what it means to be good ("a good person/good guy"), now projected onto the analyst. Given the idealization, the analyst in Jim's head can do no wrong and "gets" him perfectly. Jim also felt safe enough to start discussing various exhibitionistic sexual phantasies, i.e., his need to show his erect phallus, another getting excited by his phallus, and enjoying his excitement with him. Some of this Jim consciously connected with examples from his youth, where mutual masturbation and explorations took place.

Sexuality, wishes, and phantasies were strictly prohibited, if not taboo, in his Christian upbringing, his school, and home environment, relegating his wishes and phantasies into hiding, internally secretly. Jim's lifelong phantasy included living in a closet, looking out so he could see the world, but the world could not see him. A powerful image of closeted narcissism, although it also has a schizoid[6] feel to it.

Returning to the transference, the less conscious part of Jim would find himself tangibly restricted and inhibited if the analyst did not respond to what he brought with a keen interest or excitement, that is, perfect mirroring. Although Jim was mostly guarded and cautious about sharing his inner world in therapy (or anywhere, for that matter), the analyst's mood and state of mind were *essential in determining his openness and ability to share*.

In therapy, the analyst could, over time, venture interpretations of Jim's unique state of mind and feelings of aliveness as connected or reliant on the "sameness" of the analyst/other – specifically, the analyst/other as a needed source of vitality, mirroring, and goodness. At the same time, the analyst/other also had to feel and think similarly to allow for it to be emotionally safe to show himself. The analyst/other's mood also played a vital role in Jim's own sense of self. If the analyst/other was optimistic, open, positive, warm, and welcoming, it was safe to come out and engage. If the analyst/other was blank, neutral, or indifferent (there may be hints of this, i.e., the analyst looking tired, a bit flat, or distracted), Jim found it painful to engage, to move from the "closet."

"*Jim:* Hi! (With a handshake and nonchalance) Have you had a long day? You look tired!

Analyst: It is important to you that I'm available and attentive when we meet.

Jim: Yes, but I'm also just concerned of how you are doing.

Analyst: I appreciate your concern. And at the same time, I wonder if it may be hard for you to come in and focus on yourself, then you shift the focus onto me not to feel exposed?

Jim: That's true, but even after all these years, it still feels weird to start talking about myself. Awkward. It is what I want to do, and that's the whole point of coming here, but it's still hard. And if you look offish, I find it hard to open up.

Analyst: How you experience and see me seems to play a vital role in how you feel and govern yourself.

Jim: It is like that with my wife, too I guess. And my mother.

Analyst: Uh hum?

Jim: My wife, she's my social pillar of strength, if she's happy, I'm happy, if she's low, I'm low.

Analyst: So your sense of self is therefore tied up into her mental state.

Jim: Yes, I don't know it to be any other way."

Over time, Jim became increasingly able to focus on himself despite the rise of the aggressive self-other unit. Greater self-exploration and self-activation also brought more significant intrapsychic conflict and the need for support:

Analyst: You seem to be conflicted here. On the one hand, you long to share emotionally and simultaneously become anxious about making yourself vulnerable. You protect yourself by closing up or becoming inhibited…

Jim: It is the most scary and risky thing there is, to share, to be truly seen for all your flaws and weakness, your imperfections. There's no way I can speak about this stuff anywhere but here.

When the analyst suggested that Jim might find it possible to relate emotionally outside of therapy too, Jim returned the following session with reflections on my comment of me wanting to get rid of him or that I was insinuating treatment might end. I responded by saying how meaningful this relationship is to him and that any communication that brings separateness and mention of his individuality and authenticity threatens the relationship. This dilemma constantly ran through his relationships, and even though he had a loving wife and happy children, Jim never felt he could fully be himself. As such, Jim had to continually guard against the expression of his real needs at the risk of it conflicting with others' needs. There seems to be only room for one person's needs in his inner world and life, and it's not his! Although, for most adults, it is a reality of life to share and be supported, Jim learned throughout his development to avoid paying attention to his emotional life at all costs and resonate with his mother's. Jim learned to be perfectly in agreement (reflected in the image the other has of him) and aligned with the other's needs and feelings. Thus, there remained a constant pressure "to be" what he thinks others want him to be, versus finding and living his own authentic life.

Jim: When I speak, and someone is attentively listening and interested, it's like the warmth of a fire (holding both hands in front of him). It then feels like I have to keep the fire going, or it will go cold. They'll stop being interested; I'll bore them.

Analyst: It feels good to be heard and listened to; you feel alive and warm if there's a connection (fusion?), yet you start feeling pressure or responsibility to keep the other interested and excited; otherwise, you are of no use to them.

Jim: I also leave space for you to speak because I hate to be that person who blabbers on, when others are thinking, aagh, just shut up, will you!

Analyst: Why would what you have to say be a blabbering on?

Jim: I don't know…but I can't risk it. I have to be good, if possible *perfect at all times*, or I'll run the risk of being humiliated and scorned. I'll sometimes lie or make things up just to keep the conversation flowing, to save face.

Jim continued to work with the impact of perfectionism on his relationships and his fear of humiliation and attack valiantly, experiencing significant intrapsychic and interpersonal freedom in time.

Countertransference and the Holding of the Defensive Self of the Narcissistic Analysand

As evident in the case studies and the intrapsychic units section, the analyst working within the narcissistic dilemma may become the recipient of, or resonate through, projective identification with the various SR and OR described of the grandiose and defensive false self. Working with the fused units poses unique challenges as they remain airtight and cold anger can be evoked if the narcissistic defenses are too vigorously or directly challenged. It is challenging to tolerate and resonate with the manifest narcissistic disorder of self's need for admiration and perfect mirroring, to withhold the need not to shame the closet narcissist or eject the devaluing narcissist due to continuous devaluation. The aggressively fused unit, in turn, provides further difficulty as holding a collapsed, fragmented, and depleted self in a relationship with a devaluing attacking other remains an electrified tightrope technically. A harrowing state of mind, and although unexpected, esteem-sensitive analysand working through the abandonment depression may be at greater physical and emotional risk than other disorders of self. Masterson presents detailed process discussions in the *Emergent Self* (1993), part three, chapters 9 through 11, wherein countertransference and projective identification are discussed in supervision format, clearly illustrating the therapeutic acting out of the fused units of the impaired self of both analyst and analysand.

Notes

1 Environmental fusion that mimics the intrapsychic mother as environment fusion.
2 For Masterson, "Whether the narcissism is pathologic or healthy turns upon the quality of the sense of self-feeling and its relationship to the external object. To illustrate: If you are reading this book to glean information that will make you a better therapist and enable you to help your patients more, and you acknowledge me as the source of this information, then that is healthy narcissism. On the other hand, if you are reading the book in order to gain some knowledge that will make you feel unique and special, and you cannot acknowledge my contribution as the source of the feeling, then that is the narcissism of the exhibitionistic disorder. Finally, if you are reading this book because you have idealized me and are basking in the glow of that idealization as you read, that is the narcissism of the closet narcissistic disorder. On the other hand, to turn this around, if I wrote the book in order to teach what I have learned so that it can be used by others, and I acknowledge the importance of students to the process, that is healthy narcissism. If I wrote the book in order to exhibit my special, unique, grandiose self for perfect mirroring and do not acknowledge the student, that is exhibitionistic narcissism. Finally, if I view the audience as idealized and the source of my self-esteem, and wrote the book to gain admiration and thereby reinforce my grandiosity, that is closet narcissism" (1993, p. 13).
3 Also see the work of Rena Moses-Hrushovski (1994), *Deployment: Hiding Behind Power Struggles as a Character Defense*.
4 According to Jerry Katz (2004, in Masterson & Lieberman, 2004), the withdrawn and paranoid state of the devaluing narcissist is a continual protection against possible humiliation and shame, and not appropriation *per se*. The latter would be expected in the schizoid disorder of the self.
5 See Masterson's work of 1981, pages 16–27 as well as page 230 for a comparison between his conceptualization with that of Heinz Kohut and Otto Kernberg.
6 See Chapter 4.

Chapter 7

Separation Sensitivity and the Borderline Dilemma

As mentioned in Chapter 1, Masterson's original psychoanalytic work (1967, 1972) focussed on the residential treatment of acting-out adolescents. In securing a safe environment to contain adolescents acting out (the behavioral domain) and by providing a clear therapeutic focus and boundaries facilitating separation from the family of origin, the in-patient adolescents invariable showed symptoms of depression. That is, true to classical Freudian thinking, the management of what could not be thought, and thus expressed in acting out, finally became the focus of one of Masterson's central developmental concepts – the activation of the *abandonment depression.* More specifically, steeped in the clinical work of Margaret Mahler's developmental model, Masterson traced the borderline dilemma as a clear developmental expression of a failed separation-individuation process and the continual warding off of the abandonment depression. Clinically enabled to understand the borderline adolescent's central affective feature and interpersonal dilemma, Masterson set out to map, similarly to Kernberg and other object relations theorists, the unique endopsychic reality of the disorder.

The Split Object Relations Units of the Borderline Analysand

Immersed in the separation-individuation developmental model, Masterson (1972) soon realized the importance of *maternal libidinal availability* in supporting the evolving *True Self* of the child. Central to the developmental self and object relations approach of Masterson (1972), the borderline adolescent's dilemma was related to a borderline mother who consciously and unconsciously fostered *clinging* or

DOI: 10.4324/9781003358572-11

distancing relatedness due to her separation-individuation traumas. The latter was clearly at the expense of the child's unique individuality and natural separation-individuation needs. Synoptically, such a state of affairs is achieved through either withdrawing or punishing the child when they express separation and individuation (self-activation) needs while actively supporting regressive or enmeshed behavior (consciously or otherwise). Given the latter, the separation-individuation phase is severely stifled and much-needed autonomy strivings impaired. In essence, the borderline child is "rewarded" for not individuating and so starts an unconscious *anti-separation-individuation system* that is reflected in a specific self and object representation, ego functions, and use of defense mechanisms. It is a well-researched reality that primary maternal preoccupation and maternal libidinal availability are vital for continual ego development. As the mother of the future-separation-sensitive analysand struggles to support the separation-individuation process through acting within either a withdrawal or rewarding paradigm, the child's endopsychic world is constructed to serve the other[1] at the expense of self-activation. The withdrawing and rewarding paradigm is the foundation for the feeling of *abandonment* that becomes part of unconscious motivation and various defenses, including distancing and clinging. In Masterson's original conceptualization (1972),

> The abandonment feelings then recede into the unconscious where they lie submerged like an abscess, their overwhelming but hidden force observable only through the tenacity and strength of the defense mechanisms used to keep them in check. These defenses, however, effectively block the patient's developmental movement through the stages of separation-individuation to autonomy. He suffers from a developmental arrest.
>
> (p. 23)

Given such an endopsychic dilemma, and the reality that the borderline patient is never actively allowed to grow up (if not punished for wanting to do so!), various intrapsychic adaptations are erected against abandonment feelings. Psychoanalytically, the internalization of a withdrawing-rewarding mother creates and later reflects (or is an expression of), an internal world characterized by both a *split ego* and *split object relations unit*. Through the use of the defense mechanism of splitting, the young child, and later the adult, can effectively keep apart two contradictory primal affective states with their co-comment self and object representations. The units can be described as the *withdrawing object relations part unit* (WORU) and the *rewarding object relations part unit* (RORU) (see figure below).

Within the WORU,[2] the object representation is one of a maternal part object experienced as critical, rejecting, hostile, and angry that withdraws support and libidinal supplies in the reality of the child's positive self-assertion. The part self-representation of the WORU is characterized by painful inadequacy, helplessness, guilt, and emptiness. The linking affects are frustration, chronic anger, and resentment that mask the underlying abandonment depression.

In contrast, the RORU is characterized by a maternal part object that is loving, approving, and supportive of non-separation-individuation behavior and clinging tendencies. The part self-representation is of being a good, compliant, and passive child. The linking affect is of feeling good and being gratified, stimulating the wish for reunion:

> In terms of reality, however, both part units are pathological; it is as if the patient has two alternatives, viz., either feel bad and abandoned (the withdrawing part-unit), or feel good (the rewarding part-unit) at the cost of denial of reality and the acting out of self-destructive behavior.
>
> (Masterson, 1976, p. 63)

Given the immense emotional upheaval experienced by a withdrawing mother, ego-defenses can be viewed as inherent survival strategies against unthinkable anxieties and affect storms. Again, Mastersonian logic states that borderline defenses may be evident in separation stress[3] and/or individuation[4] strivings and stressors. This is an essential reality and frequently overlooked in general literature, especially with higher functioning borderlines; that is, not only are defenses activated by losses but also success and growth, as it would unconsciously imply separation from the primary object that will withdraw. Masterson's borderline adolescent (and adult) acts similarly to Bowlby's infants; that is, the borderline can defend against feelings of abandonment by protesting or clinging to the lost object and "expressing the wish for reunion" (Masterson, 1972, p. 35), and if the latter strategies are unsuccessful, react[5] with depression, rage, and even detachment/distancing. According to Masterson (1976), the following *distancing defenses* can

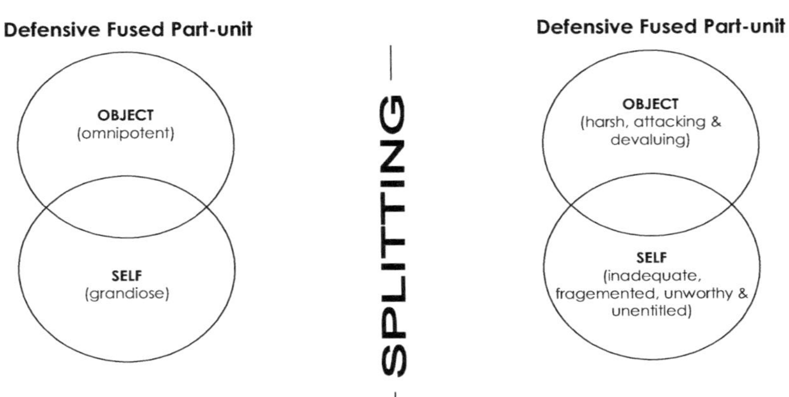

Ego Functions	Poor reality perception, impulse control, frustration tolerance and ego boundaries
Ego Defense Mechanisms	Splitting, avoidance, denial, acting-out, clinging, projection & projective identification

Figure 7.1 Split Object Relations of the Borderline Disorder of Self.

be seen in borderline adult analysand: (a) having no relationships and living in isolation, (b) exclusively having relationships with men or women who have relationships with others (affairs), (c) having deep relationships with two or more people but failing to choose and commit, (d) having spurious relationships and moving on when the relationship threatens with a need for involvement, and (e) choosing a partner that "also has anxiety about closeness and blames the conflict in the relationship on him/her" (1976, p. 77).

The Primary Therapeutic Approach to the Borderline Dilemma

The withdrawing and rewarding paradigm, resulting from a failed separation-individuation process, poses unique therapeutic challenges. According to Masterson, with its inherent neutrality, the classic psychoanalytic frame allows for the split units to become activated and worked through. This is achieved by setting very clear and definite therapeutic boundaries, clarifying the level of borderline organization (higher or lower level borderline and type), establishing clear therapeutic goals (as articulated by the patient and part of self-activation), supporting the process of continual clarification and confrontation, containing the activation of the split units, supporting the working through of the abandonment depression,[6] and scaffolding the emergence of the "Real Self" through the process of communicative matching. Given that the borderline believes that his RORU and alliance with the pathological ego is ego-syntonic, the destructive behavior needed to deny the reality of the WORU and the abandonment depression is addressed very early in the therapy. It is argued that the central therapeutic focus in the beginning phases of therapy (which could last years) is on making the alliance between the RORU and pathological ego ego-dystonic, mainly through means of *confrontation*.

Confrontation is a "*self*"*-enhancing invitation* rather than a superego-based intervention as it attempts to support the observing ego.[7,8] The aim of confrontation is ego-enhancing contact to strengthen general ego functioning to withstand the demands of character work and its transformations during the working-through phase of treatment. For Masterson,

> Confrontation is not without its own dangers. The therapist must be able to be 'really there,' empathic and 'tuned in' to the patient's feeling state in order for the confrontation to work. The confrontation

> must be faithfully wedded to the content of the patient's associations and the patient's feeling state. *It must be clearly in the patient's best interest.* If it is not, the authority inherent in the dynamic theme itself is replaced by the therapist's authority. And what might have been a useful confrontation becomes a manipulation on the part of the therapist. The therapist's chief protection against this danger is his awareness of his own feeling states and of the degree of his own narcissism. Only then can he be sure that the confrontation does not spring from his own emotions to gratify his own narcissism.
>
> (1976, p. 101) (italics added)

Masterson firmly held that confrontation should be introduced quietly, firmly, and consistently. If the clinician feels angry or contentious, it is best to take a step back and rely on the analytic observing ego, even attend supervision if necessary, "If the patient senses that the therapist is angry, he will use the anger to avoid the validity of the confrontation – i.e., the therapist is saying it because he's angry, not because it is true" (1976, p. 101). Despite a focussed and tactful approach to the analysand, resistance may be formidable given the abandonment depression. During such stalemates, Masterson recommends a certain measure of *therapeutic astonishment*,

> There is one carefully chosen exception to this rule. When resistance persists despite major confrontations and seems to be defeating therapeutic progress, a certain amount of *therapeutic astonishment* is necessary in order to alert the patient to the dangers of the tenaciousness of his resistance.
>
> (1976, p. 101)

A special note on the psychology of confrontation may suffice, as it is frequently misunderstood as attacking, criticizing, or going against the patient. The art of confrontation is very reliant on the therapist's "capacity for empathy, introspection, creativity – and understanding and knowledge" (Klein, 1989a, p. 216) to allow for the development of a "therapeutic 'echo chamber' to magnify and clarify the expression of the patient's beleaguered real self" (Klein, 1989a, p. 217). The aim of confrontation is thus as follows (Klein, 1989a, p. 220):

1. Limit setting.
2. Reality testing.

3. Clarifying the consequences of maladaptive thoughts, feelings, or behaviors.
4. Questioning the motivation for maladaptive thoughts, feelings, or behaviors.

The latter, done with care and forethought, is expected to communicate trust in the analysand's ability to take responsibility for "identifying and containing feelings, verbalizing them through sessions, and behaving in an adaptive and realistic manner" (Klein, 1989a, pp. 219–220). It is expected that limit setting will *reactivate the WORU*, which is in turn expected to *reactivate the RORU as a resistance*:

> There results a circular process, sequentially including resistance, reality clarification, working through of the feelings of abandonment (withdrawing part -unit), further resistance (rewarding part-unit) and further reality clarification, which leads in turn to further working through.
>
> (Masterson, 1976, p. 64)

It should also be mentioned that *interpretation* – the primary technique used in the working-through phase of therapy, should be seen as a *process* consisting of steps, as reflected in the abovementioned areas. The early "steps" in the interpretive process usually involve clarification and confrontation. Clarification seeks a clear understanding of the subjective experience of the analysand, bringing to the relationship areas that are repressed, unformulated, denied, and avoided. Clarification cultivates, in a non-judgmental fashion, a unique form of attentiveness with the hope of expanding awareness of thoughts, feelings, and behavior. It is thus easy to now understand that the clarification process naturally leads to the process of confrontation, another deepening of the therapy in which motivation and defense will be addressed. Again, it should be noted that it is not an adversarial approach to the analysand – it underlines the *impact* of painful reality or being *confronted by* painful reality(ies). It is a tactful, thoughtful, and even creative holding of aspects of the analysand's thoughts, feelings, and behaviors that call for further consideration and formulation. Interpretation, if needed, involves making the link between an analysand's conscious behavior, thoughts, and feelings and the possible, primarily unconscious, realities that may underly them. For Masterson, the latter should be used when the analysand *seems able to develop a transference* and be able to tolerate the affects of the working-through phase. This is important as relying on interpretation in the therapeutic acting-out phase may support the RORU defensive unit, taking over for the analysand the work that needs to be done by them, swamping their impaired self as the psychological implication of unconscious needs, wishes, and anxieties may be too engulfing or challenging to contain and reflect on, and finally, maybe a countertransference acting out (either from resonating with the OR of either the RORU or WORU). The analysand may tolerate and use a "complete" interpretation in the working-through phase due to the strengthening of the Real Self. The latter would, by definition, include a description of the significant defense, the anxiety motivating the defense, and the underlying wish, need, or fear being defended against.

In summary, it can be conceptualized that for the borderline disorder, the fundamental paradigm is the reward for regression and active withdrawal from separation-individuation, that is, self-activation. According to Masterson, "*individuation* leads to *depression* which leads to *defense*" (Masterson, 1985, p. 80) and can be conceptualized as the *borderline triad*. The borderline triad should be continually tracked and adequately addressed in psychoanalytic psychotherapy.

I now turn to a case illustrating the application of the various concepts evident in the Mastersonian model.

Case of Jessica – The Use of Distancing, Avoidance, and Focussing on the Object as a Defence[9]

Jessica, a self-referred 38-year-old Caucasian female patient, consulted the author due to a difficult separation from her partner of 9 years, "Why here? A cliché – a breakup." Since the breakup, Jessica has been re-evaluating her life, her "habits" as she calls them, and has come to the conclusion that she also needs to focus on the following realities that are linked to both the WORU and the RORU:

(a) Difficulties with intimacy as she actively pushes people away, that is, avoidance and distancing defenses, "I pushed my friends away. I have a tendency not to say what I feel; I tell people what they want to hear. The first six months are usually perfect. I don't like myself. I tend to withdraw, all hugs and kisses, and we end up being best friends. I push them away. *I also get involved with people who won't get committed; I subconsciously* know and resent it, but that is what I do. From 16, I am like this; I have had 'mother issues' since I was 16. I usually go out and party and drink to calm down. I escape reality."

(b) Pleasing other people at the expense of true self-expression.
(c) Stating and supporting her wants and needs, that is, self-activation.
(d) Managing various distancing defenses such as excessive drinking, partying, watching TV, humor, and a "poor me" attitude when experiencing stress and where avoidance doesn't seem to work.
(e) Tolerating her own emotions, especially anger, as linked with "reality" consideration and various abandonment themes.

My initial impression of Jessica was of an overwhelmed, *frightened child* who needed to hold back and seemed unsure of her own emotional realities. It later became evident that having emotions of one's own was reacted to with withdrawal and punishment. Concerning her family of origin, Jessica was the eldest of three adopted children. In the initial sessions, Jessica described a mother who would treat her children as special one minute (usually for compliance) to becoming exceptionally abusive, hostile, critical, and rejecting the next – effectively manipulating her husband and children with money and her moods. Jessica's father seemed unable to manage the affect storms and would withdraw, a behavior Jessica would later identify with:

> We were told that we were adopted and that we are special. The very next minute she would say, 'we are bastard children.' She even said my father didn't want us and if not for her. She would say such hurtful things to us. So I make people happy [RORU]. Not saying what I want [self-activation]. I have insecurity issues. It is the same in my relationship; a lot comes from my mother. Her way, and she is always right! The rest is wrong. If you have an opinion or standing up against her, she would perform, make life a misery.

Masterson's WORU and RORU units seemed painfully evident in the description. The following serve as more detailed examples of the units:

Jessica: We discussed my mother in the previous session. After the session, I asked myself, "What would I have wanted to do?" *My view doesn't matter.*

Analyst: Could you tell me more?

Jessica: Ok, it is like a seed of doubt [mother as internal object] in my mind. I want to live my life, but the seed is still there...*I do* what she wants me to do.

Analyst: How so?

Jessica: You know I told you about her knee operation. She and her boyfriend discussed it and decided, they even made a list, and there are papers they want me to sign. I should look after her! I said "no." She said, "ok, we will discuss it when we get there, face to face." I again said no. She said, "ok, I will put it aside, and you can sign later."

Analyst: You usually did what your mother asked?

Jessica: Yes, then she would treat me nicely. Her way was to buy me nice stuff. *I even do that now. If I want to say what I feel, I buy things. That is how she rewarded me.* Then I was in her good books [RORU]. We used to say our shares were up or down as long as I did what she said, and then she was nice. If I didn't, she would scream and shout at me till she got her own way. When I was about 16 or 17, she kicked me out a lot [rejection WORU]. It became a standing joke – here comes X's kid again. It would last a couple of weeks, and then I was back again.

Analyst: Where was your father?

Jessica: Well, he would come home, get a beer, and watch the grass grow, sleep at seven at night. He doesn't like confrontation; he also avoids her. He just wanted to keep the peace.

Analyst: Saying no to your mom must have been difficult; given what you have told me, how was it to say no?

Jessica: My sister said she couldn't believe I did it.

Analyst: How was it for *you to say* this to your mother?

Jessica: I totally panicked [WORU affects]. I phoned the world...my mom ended up crying and said, "you know how much I love you; you are special" [guilt and RORU]. But I know when she is being manipulative. Don't believe her. I was *angry* towards her – you know, I never stated it as strongly as I did at her. My mother has ruled my life, not allowing me to grow up – not brave enough to do what I wanted to do [self-activation and individuation]. It's not her life to lead, it's mine. I have regrets. If I had done what I wanted to do ...

Analyst: So although it seemed like your life, you were absorbed in your mother's perceptions.

Jessica: Yes!

Analyst: And you would ignore, numb, and intoxicate your feelings when you did feel.

Jessica: Yes! Since 17, I was going overboard – it was not an accident – escaping from not liking myself and being angry [negative self-representation of WORU]. It would build up. Something would happen that I should have confronted it. Builds up over weeks, and then I would vent *but not say how I feel [acting out]*. I won't say I feel hurt. I would say, "I have nothing." Actually, I mean *inside, "I feel like I am nothing"* [emptiness and void], not good enough, and angry [abandonment affects]. I feel worthless. Honestly, I feel like that most of my life. The older I got, up to five years ago, I kept it all inside. Say nothing, deal with nothing, and avoid. I am angry at me" [starts laughing]

Analyst: (Gently) Why are you laughing?

Jessica: A defensive thing – instead of saying what I truly feel.

Analyst: You started feeling, and by laughing, you push it away [avoidance as a defense].

Jessica: I don't want people to take me seriously 'cause I start to cry...I took the easy way out; that's what makes me angry. You know I have a fear of mothers! Scared that they will reject me, I feel intimidated.

Talking about the latter paradoxically led to more self-activation, "stating" and experimenting with her wants and needs in relationships, but it also re-evoked issues of fear of self-activation, avoidance, and defensive focussing on the object. The latter is part of the expected developmental course and is summarized in the algorithm of self-activation leads to anxiety that leads to defense:

Jessica: I realized I am lazy. I usually ask questions and then go with the best answer, rather than what I want to do [self-activation]. Ok, maybe lazy is not the right word; what's the word? Emotionally dependent on answers? [Looking at me expectantly – defensive focus on object.] There, I am lazy again! [Catching herself in defense.] There is no easy way to describe it [staring at me].

Therapist: Also, waiting for me to give you a word?

Jessica: [laughs] A blank one on this!

Analyst: So this is important to you, trying to find an answer for yourself, not happy about the word, and then check with me and then going blank.

Jessica: Yes, that is how it usually happens, like to mask (false self) what I think about, about important things, for me, it takes me a long time. For example, an argument, you fight with me; it will take me three days to think about it…ok… (Smiles as if aware of something)…then I *still don't do what I want to do…*

Analyst: How so?

Jessica: Don't believe in what I think, I won't say it…

In contrast to the WORU, the RORU is characterized by a maternal part object that is loving, approving, and supportive of regressive tendencies. The part self-representation is of being a good, compliant, and passive child – again, as was the case of Jessica. In an attempt to manage the latter, various distancing mechanisms were employed. Jessica's borderline defenses were constantly viewed throughout therapy as inherent survival strategies that protected her impaired real self. The separation stress (boyfriend) and various individuation strivings (standing up against her mother, making her own decisions, etc.) pressured her typical distancing and avoidant adaptations (drinking, watching TV, excessive avoidance of conflict, and so forth). Much of the fear was later linked with being rejected by her mother.

Jessica: I feel my fear is not so much the issue, that is, the fear of talking. *It is more the fear that she will reject me* (crying) [abandonment depression]. That is what I mean my shares are down. It is 80% of the fear.

Analyst: To not say what you feel is not to be rejected.

Jessica: Yes.

Jessica continued to mention her growing capacity to face her boyfriend's rejection and support herself and further notes, "*Anger is like rejection for me* [typical to many borderline patients – when

Jessica did become angry, she was most probably withdrawn from and therefore experienced rejection]. He can do what he wants so long as there is no anger. My mom is like that as well. You know this is like a child's perception! Actually, *I am one when they get angry, like a frightened little girl.* I know it sounds intense, but that is how I feel.

Jessica continued therapy and was more present in her life and its complexities. She continued to come up against the RORU and WORU as described but persevered in finding alternative and self-generated ways to short-circuit distancing and avoidant defenses.

Countertransference and the Holding of the Defensive Self of the Borderline Analysand

As evident in the case study, the analyst working within the borderline dilemma may become the recipient of, or resonate with, the projection of the various SR and OR of either the WORU or RORU as defined. The interpersonal demands of the analytic process may find the analyst unduly supporting the patient out of a feeling of wanting to "direct" the analysand's helplessness (resonating with OR of RORU) or feeling like the critically withdrawing mother by either feeling overwhelmed by the demands of the analysand or reacting with spite (resonating with the OR of the WORU). For Masterton, the *Rescue Fantasy* (1985, p. 54) is the most common countertransference reality and reflects the intensity of the abandonment depression fall-out in the environment. Masterson further believed that many structured approaches to borderline analysands (excluding the lower level, psychotic sensitive, and chronically suicidal analysands) are the product of this fantasy (see Masterson, 2000). It is also evident that the analyst may resonate with the SR of the RORU and the WORU, whereas the analysand acts out the OR part of the RORU-WORU conflict. The split units support the analyst in tracking the projection of the OR and SR, empathically identifying with the inner dilemmas the borderline analysand faces. Clinical supervision and developing an internal echo chamber to hold and process the countertransference and projective identification demands can significantly aid the analyst in sensitive and informed interventions, as discussed.

Notes

1 Clinically evident in the continuous focus on the object at the expense of the self.
2 In the thinking of Eigen (1981): "The present paper informally explores ways in which maternal abandonment gestures, especially punitive ones, threaten the integrity of mental and physical self relations and are frequently associated with suicidal urges. By punitive abandonment threats I mean the mother's active use of separation to menace and subdue the child. In certain cases, the mother may pack her own or the child's bags and mimic leaving. She may actually leave home or, worse, take the child out and leave him or her in a strange place all alone. The child learns to suppress feelings, lest the mother terrorize the child with the threat of being without her" (p. 561).
3 The latter could be due to epigenetic realities such as adolescence, midlife, and old age, trauma precipitated by, for example, having to be removed from the family/mother, illness, and so forth. The most important is to recognize the reality that separation is inevitable.
4 Also see Waska, R. (2006). *The Danger of Change. The Kleinian Approach with Patients Who Experience Progress as Trauma.* London and New York: Routledge.
5 See Masterson's (2000) borderline-diagnostic categories, that is, dependent, passive–aggressive, compulsive, and histrionic.
6 It should be noted that in short-term Mastersonian work the working through of the abandonment depression is not possible and not a central focus. Strengthening the ego and challenging the split units becomes a central focus.
7 "The observing ego will lose its awareness when the patient undergoes a regression" (Masterson, 1976, p. 101).
8 The therapeutic acting out could most easily pull the clinician into a superego position, the Master in Lacan's terms, and the reader can also review the exceptional work of Wurmser (1978, 1981) and Langs (1973, 1974, 1978a, 1980) on this matter.
9 This case was previously published in Daws, L. (2012). The Use of Distancing, Avoidance, and Focussing on the Object as Defenses in the Borderline Disorder of Self – A Mastersonian Approach. *International Journal of Psychotherapy*, 16(1), 18–29. Reprinted with permission.

Chapter 8

Conclusion and Future of the Masterson Approach

Psychoanalysis is fortunate to experience a proliferation of literature in Freudian, Kohution, Kleinian, object-relational, neuro-psychoanalytic, and attachment theory, to name a few, attesting to the inherent creativity of the human soul and the psychoanalytic tradition. As a clinician, actively reading and studying Masterson's work from the late 1950s to his last publication in 2005, one can only remain touched by Masterson's immense understanding, ability to think under clinical pressure, ability to integrate contemporary clinical and theoretical evidence into the Masterson Approach, and above all, his sincere devotion to the psychoanalytic process as guardian of the Real Self. I sincerely hope that Masterson's work remains an inspiring approach to the lifelong demands of separation-individuation, opening new and creative vistas for analysands and analysts alike. Various clinicians, both from within and from without the various Masterson Institutes and over multiple continents and languages, are integrating and elaborating on Masterson's central ideas. Their work will continue to benefit the treatment and understanding of the disorders of self and strengthen trauma-informed practice. Psychoanalytically, Masterson's work significantly adds to the theoretical and clinical contributions of luminaries such as Otto Kernberg, Heinz Kohut, and the neo-Kleinian Dr. Susan Kavaler Adler in understanding the role of mourning in the development of self. We remain indebted to his fortitude and love of psychoanalysis and the flourishing of the Real Self.

DOI: 10.4324/9781003358572-12

Bibliography

Bader, E., & Pearson, P. T. (1988). *In quest of the mythical mate: A developmental approach to diagnosis and treatment of couples therapy*. New York: Brunner Mazel.

Berg, J., & Lundh, L. G. (2022). General patterns in psychotherapists' countertransference. *Psychoanalytic Psychology*, 39(2), 145–153.

Bergman, A. (1999). *Ours, yours, mine. Mutuality and the emergence of the separate self.* Northvale, NJ: Jason Aronson, INC.

Betan, E., Heim, A. K., Conklin, C. Z., & Westen, D. (2005). Countertransference phenomena and personality pathology in clinical practice: An empirical investigation. *The American Journal of Psychiatry*, 162, 90–898.

Bleger, J. (2013). *Symbiosis and ambiguity – A psychoanalytic study*. London and New York: Routledge.

Bollas, C. (1986). *The shadow of the object. Psychoanalysis of the unthought known*. London: Free Association Books.

Bollas, C. (2012). *Catch them before they fall: The psychoanalysis of breakdown*. London and New York: Routledge.

Bollas, C. (2013). *Catch them before they fall: The psychoanalysis of breakdown*. New York: Routledge.

Bollas, C. (2015). *When the sun bursts: The enigma of schizophrenia*. New York: Yale University Press.

Brandchaft, B., Doctors, S., & Sorter, D. (2010). *Towards an emancipatory psychoanalysis. Brandchaft's intersubjective vision*. New York and London: Routledge.

Buechner, F. (1991). *Telling secrets*. San Francisco, CA: HarperCollins.

Chatham, P. M. (1985). *Treatment of the borderline personality*. New York: Jason Aronson, Inc.

Ciccone, A., & Lhopital, M. (2022). *Birth to Psychic Life*. London & New York: Routledge.

Colarusso, C. A. (2000). Separation-individuation phenomena in adulthood: General concepts and the fifth individuation. *Journal of the American Psychoanalytic Association*, 48, 1467–1489.

Cohen, M. (2003). *Sent before my time. A child psychotherapist's view of life on a neonatal intensive care unit*. London: Karnac Books.

Crastnopol, M. (2015). *Micro-trauma. A psychoanalytic understanding of cumulative psychic injury*. New York and London: Routledge.

Daws, L. (2009). Dreaming the dream: In search of endopsychic ontology. *Issues in Psychoanalytic Psychology*, 31(1), 21–40.

Daws, L. (2012). The use of distancing, avoidance, and focusing on the object as defenses in the borderline disorder of self- A Mastersonian approach. *International Journal of Psychotherapy*, 16(1), 18–29.

Daws, L. (2013). A theoretical and clinical review of various countertransference algorithms found in treating the borderline disorder of self: The Masterson tradition. *International Journal of Psychotherapy*, 17(1), 23–41.

Eigen, M. (1977). On working with "unwanted" patients. *International Journal of Psychoanalysis*, 58, 109–121.

Eigen, M. (1981). Maternal abandonment threats, mind-body relations and suicidal wishes. *Journal of the American Academy of Psychoanalysis*, 9(4), 561–582.

Eigen, M. (1986). *The psychotic core*. London: Karnac (2004).

Eigen, M. (1996). *Psychic deadness*. New York: Jason Aronson Inc.

Eigen, M. (1998). *The psychoanalytic mystic*. London: Free Association Books.

Eigen, M. (1999). *Toxic nourishment*. London: Karnac.

Eigen, M. (2001). *Damaged bonds*. London: Karnac.

Eigen, M. (2001). *Ecstasy*. Middletown, CT: Wesleyan University Press.

Eigen, M. (2002). *Rage*. Middletown, CT: Wesleyan University Press.

Eigen, M. (2004). *The sensitive self.* Middletown, CT: Wesleyan University Press.

Eigen, M. (2006). *Lust*. Middletown, CT: Wesleyan University Press.

Eigen, M. (2007). *Feeling matters*. London: Karnac.

Eigen, M., & Phillips, A. (Eds.). (1993). *The electrified tightrope*. London: Karnac (2004).

Elkin, H. (1958). On the origin of the self. *The Psychoanalytic Review*, 45, 57–76.

Elkin, H. (1972). On selfhood and the development of ego structures in infancy. *The Psychoanalytic Review*, 59, 389–416.

Eshel, O. (2019). *The emergence of analytic oneness: Into the heart of psychoanalysis*. London: Routledge.

Fairbairn's 1944 structural theory emerged from a detailed analysis of a patient's dream (see Fairbairn, 1952, pp. 95–106) - That is - I am referring to its discussion as in 1952.

Fairbairn, W. R. D. (1941). A revised psychopathology of the psychoses and the psychoneuroses. In *An object relations theory of the personality*. New York: Basic Books, 1952.

Fairbairn, W. R. D. (1952/1984). *Psychological studies of the personality*. London: Routledge & Kegan Paul.

Ferenczi, S. (1913). Stages in the development of the sense of reality. In *Sex in psychoanalysis: The selected papers of Sandor Ferenczi*, 1950 (Vol. 1) (pp. 213–239). New York: Basic Books.

Ferenczi, S. (1929). The unwelcome child and his death-instinct. *International Journal of Psychoanalysis*, 10, 125–129.

Fordham, M. (1994). *Children as individuals*. London: Free Association Books.

Fordham, M. (2019). *Explorations into the self*. London: Routledge.

Fortune, C. (2003). The analytic nursery: Ferenczi's 'wise baby' meets Jung's 'divine child.' *Journal of Analytical Psychology*, 48(4), 456–466.

Freud, S. (1914). On narcissism: An introduction. In J. Strachey (Ed.). *Standard edition*, Vol. 14 (pp. 67–102). London: Hogarth Press, 1967.

Frisch, P. (2018). *Whole therapist, whole patient: Integrating Reich, Masterson, and Jung in modern psychotherapy*. Routledge.

Galatzer-Levy, R. M. (1988). Manic–depressive illness: Analytic experience and a hypothesis. In A. Goldberg (Ed.). *Frontiers in self-psychology. Progress in self psychology* (Vol. 3) (pp. 87–102). Hillsdale, NJ: The Analytic Press.

Gomberoff, J. M., Carmen Noemi, C., & Pualuan de Gomberof, L. (1990). The autistic object: Its relationship with narcissism in the transference and countertransference of neurotic and borderline patients. *The International Journal of Psychoanalysis*, 71(2), 249–259.

Greenberg, E. (2016). *Borderline, narcissistic, and schizoid adaptations: The pursuit of love, admiration, and safety*. CreateSpace Independent Publishing Platform.

Greenspan, S. I. (1989). *The development of the ego. Implications for personality theory, psychopathology, and the therapeutic process*. Madison, CT: International Universities Press, Inc.

Grotstein, J. S. (1986). The psychology of powerlessness: Disorders of self-regulation and interactional regulation as a newer paradigm for psychopathology. *Psychoanalytic Inquiry*, 6, 93–118.

Grotstein, J. S. (1996a). Orphans of the 'Real': I. Some modern and post-modern perspectives on the neurobiological and psychosocial dimensions of psychosis and other primitive mental disorders. In J. G. Allen & D. T. Collins (Eds.). *Contemporary treatment of psychosis. Healing relationships in the "decade of the brain"* (pp. 1–26). Northvale, NJ: Jason Aronson Inc.

Grotstein, J. S. (1996b). Orphans of the 'Real': II. The future of object relations theory in the treatment of the psychosis and other primitive mental states. In J. G. Allen & D. T. Collins (Eds.). *Contemporary treatment of psychosis.*

Healing relationships in the "decade of the brain" (pp. 27–48). Northvale, NJ: Jason Aronson Inc.

Grotstein, J. S. (1997). Integrating one-person and two-person psychologies: Autochthony and Alterity in counterpoint. *The Psychoanalytic Quarterly*, 66, 403–430.

Guntrip, H. (1969). *Schizoid phenomena, object relations and the self.* New York: International Universities Press.

Hamilton, N. G. (1988). *Self and others. Object relations theory in practice.* Northvale, NJ: Jason Aronson, Inc.

Hamilton, N. G. (1996). *The self and the ego in psychotherapy.* Northvale, NJ: Jason Aronson, Inc.

Hamilton, F. J., & Masterson, J. F. (1958). Management of psychoses in general practice. *Medical Clinics of North America*, 42(3), 823–837.

Hazell, J. (Ed.). (1994). *Personal relations therapy. The collected papers of H.J.S. Guntrip.* Northvale, NJ: Jason Aronson, Inc.

Hedges, L. E. (1992). *Interpreting the countertransfrence.* Northvale, NJ: Jason Aronson.

Hedges, L. E. (1994a). *In search of the lost mother of infancy.* Northvale, NJ: Jason Aronson.

Hedges, L. E. (1994b). *Working the organizing experience: Transforming psychotic, schizoid, and autistic states.* Northvale, NJ: Jason Aronson.

Hedges, L. E. (1997). Surviving the transference psychosis. In L. E. Hedges, R. Hilton, V. W. Hilton, & O.B. Caudill, Jr. (Eds.). *Therapists at risk: Perils of the intimacy of the therapeutic relationship* (pp. 109–145). Northvale, NJ: Jason Aronson.

Hedges, L. E. (2000). *Terrifying transferences: Aftershocks of childhood trauma.* Northvale, NJ: Jason Aronson.

Heller, L., & LaPierre, A. (2012). *Healing Developmental Trauma: How Early Trauma Affects Self-Regulation, Self-Image, and the Capacity for Relationship.* North Atlantic Books.

Hollis, J. (1996). *Swamplands of the soul: New life in dismal places.* Inner City Books.

Katz, J. (2004). The schizoid personality disorder. In J. F. Masterson & A. R. Liberman (Eds.). *A therapist's guide to the personality disorders: The Masterson approach: A handbook and workbook* (pp. 91–110). Phoenix, AZ: Zeig, Tucker & Thiesen, Inc.

Kavaler-Adler, S. (1993). Object relations issues in the treatment of the preoedipal character. *American Journal of Psychoanalysis*, 53(1), 19–34.

Kavaler-Adler, S. (1995). Opening up blocked mourning in the preoedipal character. *American Journal of Psychoanalysis*, 55(2), 145–168.

Kavaler-Adler, S. (2000). *The compulsion to create: Women writers and their demon lovers.* New York: Other Press.

Kavaler-Adler, S. (2003). *Mourning, spirituality and psychic change: A new object relations view of psychoanalysis.* London: Brunner-Routledge.

Kavaler-Adler, S. (2006). "My graduation is my mother's funeral": Transformation from the paranoid-schizoid to the depressive position in fear of success, and the role of the internal saboteur. *International Forum of Psychoanalysis*, 15, 117–130.

Kavaler-Adler, S. (2007). Pivotal moments of surrender to mourning the parental internal objects. *Psychoanalytic Review*, 94, 763–789.

Kavaler-Adler, S. (2013). *The anatomy of regret: From death instinct to reparation and symbolization in vivid case studies*. London: Karnac/Routledge.

Kavaler-Adler, S. (2014). Psychic structure and the capacity to mourn: Why narcissists cannot mourn. MindConsiliums, 14(1), 1–17.

Kavaler-Adler, S. (2017). The dark side of creativity: Compulsions, blocks, and creations. MindConsiliums, 17(4), 1–29.

Kavaler-Adler, S. (2018). The beginning of heartache in character disorders: On the way to relatedness and intimacy through primal affects and symbolization. *International Forum of Psychoanalysis*, 27(4), 207–218.

Kemberg, O. (1975). *Borderline conditions and pathological narcissism*. New York: Aronson.

Khan, M. (1979). *Alienation in perversions*. London: Hogarth Press.

Khan, M. (1989). *Hidden selves: Between theory and practice in psychoanalysis*. London: Routledge.

Khan, M. (1996). *The privacy of the self: Papers on psychoanalytic theory and technique*. Karnac.

Klein, R. (1989a). The art of confrontation. In J. F. Masterson & R. Klein (Eds.). *Psychotherapy of the disorders of the self. The Masterson Approach* (pp. 215–230). New York: Brunner/Mazel.

Klein, R. (1989b). Masterson and Kohut: Comparison and contrast. In D. W. Detrick & S. P. Detrick (Eds.). *Self-psychology: Comparisons and contrasts* (pp. 311–328). Hillsdale, NJ: The Analytic Press.

Kramer, S., & Akhtar, S. (1994). *Mahler and Kohut- Perspectives on development, psychopathology, and technique*. Northvale, NJ: Jason Aronson, Inc.

Kohut, H. (1971). *The analysis of the self.* New York: International Universities Press.

Langs, R. (1973). *The technique of psychoanalytic psychotherapy* (Vol. 1). New York: Jason Aronson.

Langs, R. (1974). *The technique of psychoanalytic psychotherapy* (Vol. 2). New York: Jason Aronson.

Langs, R. (1976). *The bipersonal field*. New York: Jason Aronson.

Langs, R. (1978a). *The listening process*. New York: Jason Aronson.

Langs, R. (1978b). *Technique in transition*. New York: Jason Aronson.

Langs, R. (1979). *The supervisory experience*. New York: Jason Aronson.

Langs, R. (1980a). *Interactions: The realm of transference and countertransference*. New York: Jason Aronson.

Brooke Laufer, B. (2010). Beyond countertransference: Therapists' experiences in clinical relationships with patients diagnosed with schizophrenia (Psychosis). *Psychological, Social and Integrative Approaches*, 2(2), 163–172.

Lawson, C. A. (2000). *Understanding the borderline mother. Helping her children transcend the intense, unpredictable, and volatile relationship*. New York: Jason Aronson, Inc.

Lieberman, J. (2004). The Narcissistic personality disorder. In J. F. Masterson & A. R. Lieberman (Eds.). *A therapist's guide to the personality disorders: The Masterson approach: A handbook and workbook* (pp. 73–90). Phoenix, AZ: Zeig, Tucker & Thiesen, Inc.

Little, M. (1990). *Psychotic anxieties and containment. A personal record of an analysis with Winnicott*. New York: Jason Aronson, Inc.

Lomas, P. (1973). *True and false experience*. London: Allen Lane.

Mahler, M. (1952). On child psychosis and schizophrenia: Autistic and symbiotic infantile psychoses. In *The selected papers of Margaret S. Mahler, M.D., Vol. 1*. New York: Jason Aronson, 1979.

Mahler, M. (1961). On sadness and grief in infancy and childhood: Loss and restoration of the symbiotic love object. In *The selected papers of Margaret S. Mahler, M.D., Vol. 1*. New York: Jason Aronson, 1979.

Mahler, M. (1965). On early infantile psychosis: The symbiotic and autistic syndrome. In *The selected papers of Margaret S. Mahler, M.D., Vol. 1*. New York: Jason Aronson, 1979.

Mahler, M. (1966). Notes on the development of basic moods: The depressive affect. In *The selected papers of Margaret S. Mahler, M.D., Vol. 2*. New York: Jason Aronson, 1979.

Mahler, M. (1967). On human symbiosis and the vicissitudes of individuation. In *The selected papers of Margaret S. Mahler, M.D., Vol. 2*. New York: Jason Aronson, 1979.

Mahler, M. (1971). A study of the separation-individuation process—And its possible application to borderline phenomena in the psychoanalytic situation. *The Psychoanalytic Study of the Child*, 26, 403–424.

Mahler, M. (1972a). On the first three subphases of the separation-individuation process. In *The selected papers of Margaret S. Mahler, M.D., Vol. 2*. New York: Jason Aronson, 1979.

Mahler, M. (1972b). Rapprochement subphase of the separation-individuation process. In *The selected papers of Margaret S. Mahler, M.D., Vol. 2*. New York: Jason Aronson, 1979.

Mahler, M. (1974). Symbiosis and individuation: The psychological birth of the human infant. In *The selected papers of Margaret S. Mahler, M.D., Vol. 2*. New York: Jason Aronson, 1979.

Mahler, M. S. (1979a). *The selected papers of Margaret S. Mahler. Volume 1. Infantile psychosis and early contributions*. New York: Jason Aronson.

Mahler, M. S. (1979b). *The selected papers of Margaret S. Mahler. Volume 2. Separation-Individuation*. New York: Jason Aronson.

Mahler, M. S., & Furer, M. (1960). Observations on research regarding the "symbiotic syndrome" of infantile psychosis. In *The selected papers of Margaret S. Mahler, M.D., Vol. 1*. New York: Jason Aronson, 1979.

Mahler, M. S., & Gosliner, B. J. (1955). On symbiotic child psychosis: Genetic, dynamic, and restitutive aspects. *The Psychoanalytic Study of the Child*, 10, 195–214.

Mahler, M. S., Pine, F., & Bergman, A. (1975). *The psychological birth of the human infant: Symbiosis and individuation*. New York, NY: Basic Books.

Mahler, M. S., & McDevitt, J. B. (1982). Thoughts on the emergence of the sense of self, with particular emphasis on the body self. *Journal of the American Psychoanalytic Association*, 30(4), 827–848.

Manfield, P. (1992). *Split self/split object: Understanding and treating borderline, narcissistic, and schizoid disorders*. New York: Jason Aronson Press, Inc.

Margolis, B. (1986). Joining, mirroring, psychological reflection: Terminology, definitions, theoretical considerations. *Modern Psychoanalysis*, 11, 19–35.

Masterson, J. F. (1967). *The psychiatric dilemma of adolescence*. Boston: Little Brown.

Masterson, J. F. (1972). *Treatment of the borderline adolescent. A developmental approach*. New York: Wiley-Interscience.

Masterson, J. F. (1976). *Psychotherapy of the borderline adult: A developmental approach*. New York: Brunner/Mazel.

Masterson, J. F. (1978). *New perspectives on psychotherapy of the borderline adult*. New York: Brunner Mazel.

Masterson, J. F., & Lu Costello, J. (1980). *From borderline adolescent to functioning adult- the test of TIME*. New York: Brunner/Mazel Publishers.

Masterson, J. F. (1981). *The narcissistic and borderline disorders: An integrated developmental approach*. New York and London: Routledge.

Masterson, J. F. (1983). *Countertransference and psychotherapeutic technique*. New York: Brunner/Mazel.

Masterson, J. F. (1985). *The real self. A developmental, self, and object relations approach*. New York: Brunner/Mazel, Inc.

Masterson, J. F. (1988). *The search for the real self. Unmasking the personality disorder of our age*. New York: The Free Press.

Masterson, J. F. (1993). *The emerging self. A developmental, self, and object-relational approach to the treatment of the closet narcissistic disorder of the self*. New York: Brunner/Mazel publishers.

Masterson, J. F. (2000). *The personality disorders: A new look at the developmental self and object relations approach, theory, diagnosis, and treatment*. Phoenix, AZ: Zieg, Tucker, & Heisen.

Masterson, J. F. (Ed.). (2005). *The personality disorders through the lens of attachment theory and the neurobiologic development of the self. A clinical integration*. Phoenix, AZ: Zeig, Tucker & Thiesen, Inc.

Masterson, J. F., & Costello, J. L. (1980). *From borderline adolescent to functioning adult: The test of time: A follow-up report of psychoanalytic psychotherapy of the borderline adolescent and family*. New York: Brunner/Mazel, Publishers.

Masterson, J. F., & Klein, R. (1989). *Psychotherapy of the disorders of the self. The Masterson Approach*. New York: Brunner/Mazel.

Masterson, J. F., & Klein, R. (1995). *Disorders of the self. New therapeutic horizons. The Masterson Approach*. New York: Brunner/Mazel.

Masterson, J. F., & Lieberman, A. R. (2004). *A therapist's guide to the personality disorders. The Masterson Approach. A handbook and workbook*. Phoenix, AZ: Zeig, Tucker & Thiesen, Inc.

Masterson, J. F., Tolpin, M., & Sifneos, P. E. (1991). *Comparing psychoanalytic psychotherapies. Developmental, self, and object relations. Self psychology. Short term dynamic*. New York: Brunner/Mazel publishers.

Mendelsohn, R. M. (1987a). *The I of consciousness: Development from birth to maturity* (Vol. 1). New York and London: Plenum Medical Book Company.

Mendelsohn, R. M. (1987b). *It all depends on how you look at it: Development of pathology in the cohesive disorders* (Vol. 2). New York and London: Plenum Medical Book Company.

Mendelsohn, R. M. (1987c). *Believing is seeing: Pathology of development in the non-cohesive disorders* (Vol. 3). New York and London: Plenum Medical Book Company.

Mendelsohn, R. M. (1987d). *The principles that guide the ideal therapist* (Vol. 4). New York and London: Plenum Medical Book Company.

Moses-Hrushovski, R. (1994). *Deployment: Hiding behind power struggles as a character defense*. Northvale, NJ: Jason Aronson Inc.

Orcutt, C. (2012). *Trauma in personality disorders: A clinician's handbook- The Masterson Approach*. Bloomington, IN: AuthorHouse.

Orcutt, C. (2021). *The unanswered self: The Masterson Approach to the healing of personality disorders*. London: Karnac.

Pearson, J. (1995). Mirrors of rage: The devaluing narcissistic patient. In J. F. Masterson & R. Klein (Eds.). *Disorders of the self: New therapeutic horizons: The Masterson approach* (pp. 299–312). New York: Brunner/Mazel, Publishers.

Pearson, J. (2004). The Masterson approach to differential diagnosis. In J. F. Masterson & A. R. Liberman (Eds.). *A therapist's guide to the personality disorders: The Masterson approach: A handbook and workbook* (pp. 35–54). Phoenix, AZ: Zeig, Tucker & Thiesen, Inc.

Perry, J. W. (1953). *The self in psychotic process. Its symbolization in schizophrenia*. Berkeley and Los Angeles: University of California Press.

Perry, J. W. (1974). *The far side of madness*. Dallas, TX: Spring Publications, Inc.

Rinsley, D. B. (1982). *Borderline and other self-disorders*. New York: Aronson.

Rinsley, D. B. (1989). *Developmental pathogenesis and treatment of borderline and narcissistic personalities*. Northvale, NJ: Jason Aronson, Inc.

Roberts, D. D., & Roberts, D. S. (2007). *Another chance to be real: Attachment and object relations treatment of borderline personality disorder*. New York and London: Jason Aronson Press, Inc.

Scharff, D. E., & Scharff, J. S. (1991). *Object relations couple therapy*. Northvale, NJ: Jason Aronson, Inc.

Schore, A. N. (1994). *Affect regulation and the origins of the self. The neurobiology of emotional development*. Hillsdale, NJ: Lawrence Erlbaum Associates.

Schore, A. N. (2003a). *Affect regulation and the repair of the self*. New York: W.W. Norton & Company.

Schore, A. N. (2003b). *Affect dysregulation and the disorders of the self*. New York: W.W. Norton & Company.

Searles, H. F. (1965). *Collected papers on schizophrenia and related subjects*. New York: International Universities Press.

Searles, H. (1979). *Countertransference and related subjects*. New York: International Universities Press.

Sechehaye, M. (1951a). *Symbolic realization*. New York: International Universities Press.

Sechehaye, M. (1951b). *Autobiography of a schizophrenic girl*. New York: Grune & Stratton.

Seinfeld, J. (1991). *The empty core: An object relations approach to psychotherapy of the schizoid personality*. New York: Aronson.

Settlage, C. F. (2001). *Three faces of mourning. Melancholia, Manic defense, and moving on*. Northvale, NJ: Jason Aronson, Inc.

Shengold, L. (1989). *Soul murder: The effects of childhood abuse and deprivation*. New Haven, CT: Yale University Press.

Spotnitz, H. (1969). *Modern psychoanalysis of the schizophrenic patient*. New York: Grupe & Stratton.

Spotnitz, H. (1985). *Modern psychoanalysis of the schizophrenic patient: Theory of the technique*. New York: Human Sciences Press.

Stern, D. N. (1985). *The interpersonal world of the infant: A view from psychoanalysis and developmental psychology*. New York: Basic Books.

Sullivan, H. S. (1953). *The collected works of Harry Stack Sullivan. Volume 1 and 2*. New York: W.W. Norton and Company.

Sullivan, H. S. (1948). Meaning of anxiety in psychiatry and in life. *Psychiatry*, 11, 1–13.

Summers, F. (2005). *Self creation. Psychoanalytic therapy and the art of the possible*. Hillsdale, NJ: The Analytic Press, INC.

Suttie, I. D. (1935). *The origins of love and hate*. London: Kegan Paul, Trench, Trubner & Co., LTD.

Solan, R. (2015). *The enigma of childhood*. London: Karnac.

Tustin, F. (1981/2013). Psychological birth and psychological catastrophe. In *Autistic states in children* (pp. 96–110). New York: Routledge.

Van Buren, J., & Alhanati, S. (2010). *Primitive mental states. A psychoanalytic exploration of the origins of meaning*. London: Routledge.

Willliams, G. (1998). *Internal landscapes and foreign bodies: Eating disorders and other pathologies*. London: Routledge (Tavistock Clinic Series).

Williams, P. (2010). *The fifth element*. London: Karnac Books.

Williams, P. (2013). *Scum*. London: Karnac Books.

Winnicott, D. W. (1945). Primitive emotional development. *International Journal of Psychoanalysis*, 26, 137–143.

Winnicott, D. W. (1958). The capacity to be alone. *International Journal of Psychoanalysis*, 39, 416–420.

Winnicott, D. W. (1969). The use of an object. *International Journal of Psychoanalysis*, 50, 711–716.

Winnicott, D. W. (1974). Fear of breakdown. *International Review of Psycho-Analysis*, 1, 103–107.

Wurmser, L. (1978). *The hidden dimension. Psychodynamics in compulsive drug use*. New York: Jason Aronson.

Wurmser, L. (1981). *The mask of shame*. London: The John Hopkins University Press, Ltd.

Index

Page numbers in *italic* denote figures.

Milton Keynes UK
Ingram Content Group UK Ltd.
UKHW022010170124
436223UK00014B/88